QUICK CONTENT FORMULA

Get Unlimited Ideas & In 5 Minutes You Can Create Great Blog Posts, Articles, & Newsletter Emails

By Richard N. Stephenson

This book is about coming up with unlimited ideas and the absolute quickest way to get them polished and out to an interested audience.

I0494033

TABLE OF CONTENTS

WHAT IS THE QUICK CONTENT FORMULA (QCF)?

I've been doing this internet thing for a long time. As a matter of fact, while my first website was born in the late 1990's, my first real blog was born in the early second half of 2010. In internet time, I'm an old fogey who's been messing around with code and computers for a long time and blogging has changed my world.

But boy have things changed!

The ability to just jump into a platform like WordPress, put in my content, make it look nice, and then have this beautiful article that's viewable by the world is remarkable. To top it off, I can change the look and feel at the press of a button. This is simply amazing considering my main tool used to be Microsoft Notepad. Uggg.

Let's go through the **What It's All About** portion of the book so you can get an understanding of why I want you to never ever write another blog post, article, or newsletter email the same way again and still get more readers, be more successful, and maintain your sanity.

As a matter of fact, after you master the Quick Content Formula, your biggest problem will be coming up with practical, doable, and fun things to write about. That's exactly the reason the first part of this book is about making you an idea finding ninja.

This book is about coming up with unlimited ideas and the absolute quickest way to get them polished and out to an interested audience.

Here's what the Quick Content Formula does for you:

1) You Can Create Unlimited Blog Content With Greater Speed

If you've been blogging for more than a month, then I know that you've sat down at your computer at the last couple of hours of Sunday evening with that little cursor blinking at you. That tiny group of vertical pixels taunting you and making you curse the electrons that are flowing to your screen.

It's a horrible feeling.

Some people call it writer's block, but that doesn't matter here. What matters is you are in a bind to produce content on a schedule that either you've set up for yourself or that your readers have come to expect. It's a horrible feeling to not express what you're thinking or even to know what to talk about.

What if you could do a little research upfront, have a list of things to talk about, and then within 5 minutes have an entire 600 word blog post draft done? Sounds too good to be true?

Typing up a blog post used to take me an hour and a half to get that first 600 words and then another 30 minutes to an hour to make it look presentable. Forget about doing 2 or 3 posts in a day, that's just too much work. But does it have to be?

If you fully utilize dictation, transcription, and ninja tools to make it all work better, then you will transform the way you do your blogging and content generation. The speed is amazing.

I'll get into it later in the book, but there are times when I can do **9,000 to 12,000 words (about 36 to 48 pages in Microsoft Word) in one hour** using a bulk processing method.

That's *15, 600 word blog posts in an hour*, my friend.

2) You Can Create a Great First Draft

I don't want anyone to get illusions of grandeur here. These dictation runs are going to be decent articles you're producing by this 5 minute Quick Content Formula, but they'll need a little massaging before you release them.

Until you have a ton of practice at it, being able to come up with a ready-to-go article is going to be pretty tough. Even after hundreds of dictated articles, you're still going to have to do some type of editing and presenting to make it look good for the folks out there... just like any draft.

Know that whatever you dictate is going to be a *good first draft*. There's no intention to publish it right away, and I suggest several layers of revision after that just like you would a standard written post.

Go into this method expecting to do pretty crappy at first. It's okay though as all first drafts suck. Successful author of the Dresden Files series of fiction books, **Jim Butcher**, said so himself on his personal writing blog and I believe it.

3) You Can Create Great Technical Drafts

I had a bit of a dilemma with this book. A lot of it has technical aspects that require me to go off and get exact website clicking paths, URL's, make tables, and get specific chunks of data. There's no way I could have easily rattled off these technical bits in an accurate fashion via dictation.

However, I am approaching this book as a hybrid. The sections that are predominantly informative text are pretty easy to dictate out (like these first few chapters here). After it's been transcribed I will come back and then add the tables, the links, the references, the research, and the other things that support what I'm talking about.

Know that you won't be able to do super-complex, detailed articles, or books in one pass. However, you can get a great pre-technical draft going and a pretty dog-gone good draft at that.

Now, Take Your Efforts to New Levels

The whole purpose you're trying to get here is to create unlimited blog content with greater speed, to create good first drafts, and to have something to work with. Oh yeah and to kill that stupid little blinking cursor and have content to deliver to the world.

WHY USE THE QCF?

I know what you're thinking. You probably don't know too much about dictation, maybe even less about transcription, and aren't sure about the process I'm writing about. Well, that's good as this is the right book for you.

I am giving you step-by-step instructions. You won't need to guess, just produce.

I will cover everything you need to know in simple, easy terms, supplying the no-to-minimal cost route as well as the much quicker, much more effective, slightly more complex, and slightly more expensive route. You choose which works best for you so long as you commit to producing some great content for the world.

I know I started off boot-strapping and going as cheaply and quickly as possible. I eventually moved up to putting the resources that I have an abundance of into the resources I am lacking. What that means is I started using the money coming in to make up for the time I didn't have. I'll never get that time back. Ever.

Here are four different reasons why you should want to power through the Quick Content Formula and make this a staple in your content generation plan.

1) Stand Out From The Crowd

Who do you know that is able to generate 15, conversationally toned, 600 word blog posts in 1 hour? No one? If you do, there's no doubt they're using some form of the QCF.

In traditional blog post or letter writing methods, people will do their first draft, come back for another edit, then come back to make it nicer sounding, and finally again to add extra layers of conversational tone and friendliness.

But what I've seen, is that dictating your articles through the thoughts that are flowing out of you automatically sets you in a conversational tone. This is especially true if you're excited and you picture your audience while you're dictating. Don't laugh - it works.

Also, just think if you could actually use the audio you're creating in another form of client, reader, or subscriber gift. What if you could turn one simple 5 minute recording into several different offerings in addition to the text that's coming out of the transcription? Leverage, my friend. I'll get into this powerful concept later.

Plus, this leveraged content will automatically have that warmth and personal touch that comes with the audio or spoken format. This is an immediate touch of branding, friendliness, and communication that isn't found at all of the me-too bloggers. Stand out from the crowd. It's noisy out there and they need to hear your voice.

2) Catch Up To The Elite And Surpass The Hobbyists

You may have friends or people that you follow that post once a week, once a month, or a few times a year. What if you spent 1 hour today, 2 hours on the weekend, and maybe a couple more hours over the next week and created all the posts you'll need to post 3 times a week for the next five months?

That's right, just 5 hours. Not consecutive, just in your free time dictating messages and articles. That relatively little chunk of time will have your blog in autopilot mode for the next third to half of the year. It's amazingly freeing and allows you to work on other projects while your blog still grows.

If you wanted to, you could keep stacking stuff on top. I know at one point in time earlier in 2013, I was posting 4 and 5 articles a day just because I had so much content and was so excited about getting stuff out there. We'll talk about frequency and how much you want to bug your readers a little bit later in the book.

3) Grow Your Business, Blog, & Audience

If you're just starting out, Google doesn't know you, Google doesn't love you, and nobody in the world knows you exist. But what if you could jumpstart your blogging career and "being noticed" factor by a year or a year and a half?

What if you could release 50 good articles right away and then have another 60 scheduled for every day for the next month and a half? What if you use that next month and a half to build up more posts for the following months?

You immediately have about 110 posts already out there available to be found by Google, interested people, and the whole world. I think you can see that this beats the trajectory of the "once a week" or "once a month" blogger starting from scratch.

What could be 12 posts a year, or 52 posts a year, can quickly balloon into several hundred posts a year or even every couple of months, depending on how much you want it.

All of these posts are pointers and leads back to you. This is your ultimate expression of how you want to help the world and maybe make some more money. There's also this theory and idea that I really like called the *luck surface area*. Hat tip to **Jason Roberts** for this idea, though I'm fitting it for the QCF.

Every piece of content you put out there is a small percentage of a chance of you being found. Let's just call it a "piece of luck." Picture an archer shooting arrows at a target. The more pieces of luck you have out there, the bigger your target gets and the easier it is for the archer to land a shot. Let's assume a 'shot' is a good thing for this example.

Well, what if you have a hundred pieces of luck out there? Wouldn't you say your target area or surface area of being found grows? What about 200 pieces? 500? 1,000? The bigger you grow, the *better chance of luck* hitting your target.

4) Practice Speaking, Flowing And Being Fluid

When I first started out with this, I couldn't get an article under five minutes with all the points I wanted to talk about. Don't get me wrong, there are still days when I have a tough time and I'd have to do quite a bit of magic in audio post-production processing to get it where I need it to be.

However, I've gotten so much better at being able to cut back on the verbal filler. I'm talking about getting rid of the extra 'um', 'so', and 'and' flubs all over the place. I also majorly cut down on the completely awful run-on sentences. With practice, you begin to see where you need help in what you're saying and how to better form your ideas off the cuff.

This process eventually becomes a **state of 'flow'** for you. This state of flow begins to be a habit that you can jump right into when it comes time to do it next time. It'll take some practice, but it's a wonderful thing. It could lead into speaking or other face-to-face methods of content delivery you've been dreading before (like YouTube videos).

Why Wouldn't You Use The QCF?

The QCF method of creating awesome content at breakneck speeds and unlimited potential is something you really need to consider. It'll help you stand out from the crowd, you'll be able to catch up to those ahead of you, and surpass those that just aren't as serious enough. You'll grow your business, blog, and audience at awesome levels. And hey, you'll become more fluid in your speaking and thoughts.

Can you really afford not to build all these skills just by one little 5-minute talk into a recorder? Let's go talk a little bit more about my proof and end results with this method.

MY PROOF

I took on this idea of transcribing in bulk to create good content at awesome speeds because there are some days I just don't feel like typing. I also had the idea that the 20 to 30 minute drive to wherever I need to be on any given day is pretty much wasted.

Sure, I can fill that drive time with podcasts and audio books to listen to. A lot of times I do just that. However, sometimes you just have to turn off that "consumer mode" and go into "**producer mode**." Make stuff instead of take stuff.

Could you imagine if you had a 30 minute commute one way, five days a week, to work? What you could do with those 5 hours of content generating potential? Did you know that most audio books range in the 3-8 hour length timeframe?

Yes, we're talking you could potentially make 1 to 2 audio books every month or every couple of weeks, depending on how much you want it. That's pretty awesome just to think about.

Now, if you turn that "producing time" into 5 minute articles, we're talking hundreds of articles per month. Remember, this was just time that was usually wasted listening to a bunch of crazy people screaming on the radio or honking at each other in traffic.

Life-shatteringly amazing.

I've leveraged my free time by taking advantage of the QCF method. I know that my increasing ability to produce content and assets that point back to me is important in this evolving digital era. I know that my growing desire to add more value to other people's lives is a benefit for everyone and motivation to continue on.

Before I get too mushy over here, I have a feeling you could benefit from seeing a few hard, cold numbers to see what's possible. Here's some of the proof I have that I think you'll appreciate. I hope it will inspire you to take the Quick Content Formula method on and give it a try.

1) Google Numbers Over The Past Few Years

At the end of 2010, I had 57 posts on my main site, richardstep.com. Not too impressive, but I was doing okay. I was randomly blogging about crazy stuff and I didn't really have a focus.

The more and more I learned, the more I decided to focus on stuff that was important to me for 2011. By the end of 2011, my total post count was 135, a little bit better, but still left a lot to be wanting. That was only 78 posts that year after all.

Now there's an important point to note here. I went into "super consumer mode" and *read 213 books in 2011*. I just went completely crazy, and some of my posting and creating articles suffered because of it. Here's a list of the books if you're curious (it includes ratings and recommendations):

http://richardstep.com/self-help/213-good-books-read/

Oh yeah, my wife and I welcomed our lovely infant daughter into the world. She took some time and attention, too! Her brother was about 3 years old then and was such a great helper. But back to *this* book...

I was still able to get out posts on a regular basis using the old "fret over the blinking cursor" method. This was about the time I created my own self-test for finding personal strengths. Let's just say I started using my strengths to the fullest. Here's the free test if you're interested:

http://richardstep.com/strengths-fulltest/

In 2012, I went into producer mode and *wrote 7 books* while posting articles on a regular basis, as well as other projects that required a lot of personal touch time. As you can see, my total blog count for the end of 2012 was 223. Still pretty decent and moving along, but nothing to brag to my mom about.

It was in early 2013 that I decided to just off the cuff record my thoughts on family, parenting, faith, and success every night for the course of 30 days. I did this and started to transcribe them all myself. I put all of these transcriptions together in a little report that I gave away to my blog subscribers some time ago.

Let's just say the final product was just *okay*. It wasn't the greatest thing I've ever put together, but it was okay. Remember, I was doing it off the cuff, no planning, no real goal, and no real direction. The QCF wasn't realized fully, yet.

However, the experience did prove to me that this process of producing dictated content was pretty cool. But there was one thing that I found out I really didn't enjoy. I was not a big fan (at all!) of transcribing my own stuff for a couple of reasons:

1) It would take me a very long time
2) There's just something weird about hearing myself talk to myself

I highly recommend that when you take this QCF method on, you transcribe at least your first couple of dictations before you seek any other method. This *will* help you see what it's like from the transcription-side of the process. It's a very important part, but not necessarily one to dwell on.

Back to the point. In early 2013 I stumbled upon what has now become my go-to method for creating quick articles or rough draft content for things that I want to put out there.

It was in the early 2013 timeframe when I just went completely off the wall crazy with what I would soon dub the Quick Content Formula. Here's a breakdown of my posting frequency - you tell me when I started using the QCF:

JAN 2013 = 11 posts
FEB 2013 = 17 posts
MAR 2013 = 6 posts
APR 2013 = 47 posts
MAY 2013 = 77 posts
JUN 2013 = 29 posts
JUL 2013 = 31 posts
AUG 2013 = 23 posts

Pretty obvious, right? Also, as of writing this sentence, I have another 16 posts scheduled out to give me plenty of time to work on this book and a few other major projects.

This brings my total post count thus far in August of 2013 to **463** published posts. That's more than double all posts done in 2010, 2011, and 2012 combined. I've also written 4 books (in addition to this one) since April 2013. The QCF works my friend.

2) Traffic Numbers, En Masse

Let's dive into a little bit more of the outcomes most people are looking for: comments, viewers, readers, and traffic. You've seen some of my numbers already, but let's go into the higher level generic approach that a new content producer can think about too.

What if you were able to come up with long tail keywords or phrases that people were looking for and create content around those? What if you knew that those key terms you're using would get about one view per day? Not too much - nothing to go home and brag about. That is, until you multiply your efforts and go big.

What happens to your blog when you release another 200, 1-view-a-day posts? You have 200 new views a day and that's quite a bit bigger deal. Also, what you'll find out is that somewhere between 1% and 2% of your posts will be knockout hits that get a whole lot more attention than you expect.

I'm talking about unexpected results to be proud of here like 10, 20 and 30 fold your normal traffic. For now, just think about the base number of 1-view-per-day so you don't get too excited. The overall point here is the more you create, the more eyeballs you can help bring to your website.

3) Feeling, Motivation And Fun

It's so much more fun to ignore that blinking cursor and just talk what I want to say into a microphone. I can actively create a mental picture of the tons of awesome content that I can create with a whole lot less effort and in a whole lot more friendly style.

When it comes to me knowing that my 45 scheduled posts are just about all published and it's time for another wave of content, I'm motivated. I go to that state of mind, I make my little cheat sheet index cards or images on my phone, I read through them, and I dictate as I go.

I normally do 15 posts an hour and I can stop right there. BOOM! I've got the next 15-30 days' worth of blog posts covered, depending on how I want to spread it out. Piece of cake!

No fretting, no messing, no nothing to get me all hot and bothered. It's just an hour of my time that would have been spent writing *only* 600 words via the old, non-QCF method. Instead, I created 15 of those 600 words posts. That's 9,000 words an hour. That's a great feeling.

4) Money, Money, Money

However you monetize your blogging or writing efforts all come down to the fact that you need eyeballs. I run ads, I have products, I have affiliate offers, and I have a whole bunch of different funnels leading people towards products and offerings that I know will be useful for them and they might even invest a little cash in.

But I have to mention a really awesome event that happened shortly after I started blasting out all these articles. I did some long tail keyword research and came up with some pretty good articles about general business ideas.

By the way, that was another problem I had - not enough good, proven, and useful blog post ideas. Don't worry; we tackle the hee-haw out of that problem in this book. Back to the story.

I picked the long tail, low traffic keywords that weren't getting a whole lot of attention. Well, it just so happened that one of the posts had to do with conference meeting icebreakers. This was a post that detailed a couple little ideas on games or things that groups of people could do in a corporate environment to help start off a meeting in a fun, friendly manner.

As my "call to action" at the end of that article I said, "hey, the best idea you could do is to go checkout the *DOPE Bird Personality Test* and try it out as an ice breaker. You can have fun and you can understand each other better."

I didn't pay any special attention to it and I just got back to work on other projects. The DOPE Bird Personality Test is one of the **career and personal development products** I have available, so it was a logical progression from the content of the article. It was something I thought would be genuinely valuable to people reading that article.

Not more than a couple days after that post was published (or the time it took Google to index the post), I had someone email me about a bulk purchase of the test to use as an icebreaker for their upcoming conference meeting.

Now, this was a pretty substantial order of $1,992.50 for a post that I literally took five minutes to dictate. I've said it before and I'll say it again, increase your luck surface area and these kind of things start to happen.

Time to Make Your Own Proof

We all like proof, we all like numbers, and we like to see that new methods are actually working for people before we decide to take them on. I hope that the data and story I've provided from my personal experience has helped build your confidence in the QCF for your own efforts.

The chances of life-shattering failure through creation of more awesome content is little to none. The upside potential for success by creating a ton of useful content is only limited by your recording device's memory card, your vocal cords, and your drive to get stuff done.

Get 'er done.

PART 1

UNLIMITED IDEAS

BECOME A BRAINSTORMING MASTER

There's nothing worse than sitting in front of the computer and not having anything to write about. The more you scramble to find a topic without any type of guiding direction, the more frustrating the process becomes. This can quickly turn your side business or fun hobby into one heck of a chore.

Forget all of that forever.

You want ideas? I mean an unlimited stream of proven, useful, and straight-forward ideas right here right now? Good. Stick around as there are a few great ways to come up with more ideas than you can shake a stick at. People still say that, right?

I'm going to present you with the most "tool and skill" *independent* method first: brainstorming. Sure, it helps to have experience with thinking creatively about things, but these brainstorming tools can be picked up by anyone at any time *without* an internet connection.

I highly recommend a piece of paper and writing utensil or white board and markers for the following brainstorming tactics. Yes, you can use a text editing or word processing program if you must. Sheesh.

As a quick note, I will go into a few more concrete, internet-savvy methods after this. Also, I am trying to present as much as I can in a free or low-cost manner because no amount of convincing will turn a boot-strapper over to the paid-side until they do it themselves and see the light.

However, I do include tips related to software-assisted methods that most won't jump into right away. I totally understand that and I was there for a long time. Speaking of time, that'll be the biggest deciding factor in which route you ultimately end up adopting. The only resource you never get back is time. Okay, let's move on.

Oh and just in case you're wondering why I'm going to spend a chunk of the book talking about ideas, then let me tell you. You'll be producing content so fast that having ideas will become your biggest problem. We're going to fix that *right now*.

Fears, Needs, & Wants

What do people really care about? Themselves. At the end of the day (and at the beginning for that matter), El Numero Uno is the first thing on the mind of your viewers, subscribers, and clients. Sure, some of them may have more outward facing goals to accomplish, but there is always base human psychology that no one can get away from.

We have fears.
We have needs.
We have wants.

These are deeply-rooted, internal, and powerful triggers inside of all of us that bring out the most quick, motivated, and decisive actions in everyone. These are the human "hot buttons" that come installed at birth. Okay well technically only the fear of falling and the fear of loud noises are installed at birth, but you get my drift.

Speak, focus on, and target your content about these things and you will have content that matters. You will have content that is relevant, timeless, and useful for those seeking it. The keys to success are providing value to those who cross your path. Focus on these topics and make them work for your goals.

Here are time-tested and universal fears, needs, and wants for most human beings.

Fears:
- Death
- Failure
- Success
- Isolation
- Loss of Self-Dominance
- Rejection
- The Unknown
- Enclosed spaces
- Flying
- Heights
- Intimacy
- Public Speaking
- Commitment

Needs:
- Affection
- Creation
- Freedom
- Identity
- Protection
- Subsistence
- Understanding
- Clothing
- Shelter
- Food, Air, Water
- Health and Well Being
- Family and Friends

Wants:
-Abundance of Money
-Attraction of Others
-Sex Appeal and Appearances
-Business Opportunities
-Food Satisfaction
-Good Health
-More Leisure Time
-Recognition
-Success and Wealth
-Ultimate Comfort
-Self Actualization
-Finding and Living Purpose
-Respect
-Self Esteem and Confidence

How exactly should you use this information? Simple. Fear is usually the strongest motivator though I don't recommend focusing directly on the fear for everything you do. For the sake of the example, let's stick with fear.

Pick "fear of success" for example. What do you think this means to the average person? What are the 3 to 5 main characteristics that make up a person who has a deep-seeded fear of anything success or wealth oriented?

As an example, consider a fearful, success-averse mindset that embraces:

1) Frugality
2) Risk aversion
3) Scarcity
4) Lack of confidence
5) Desire to consume as oppose to create

Take these 5 characteristics of the fear of success and turn them into something that matters to your target audience. Break each one of them down into a 'topic' and talk about how to provide a solution to that problem, geared toward your target audience.

For instance, you can focus on helping corporate cube-dwellers learn risk mitigation and control so they feel confident enough to make business experimentation a bigger part of their lives.

But it doesn't stop there. That is just a guiding principle and focus for the content you plan to generate. Now you can dive into the many step-by-step methods to bust the cube-dweller risk-aversion habit with deeper tools.

Here are a few to whet your grind-stone. Let's start off with an easy one.

Idea Grid Brainstorming

You've already thought a bit about your topic, your target audience, and how you can help them solve a specific problem. Now let's assign some characteristics to that topic and audience, flip them up and around, and see what new ideas come out. This method of brainstorming is great for coming up with quick and simple ideas without much thought required.

Let's select "staying motivated at work" as our main topic and jump right into the steps.

Idea Grid Steps:

1. Write down your topic in a brief question form (the human brain loves to answer questions).

ex) How can I stay motivated at work?

2. Write down 3-5 important characteristics or qualities of the topic. These are things you *think* affect the question in some way. They don't have to be facts, just good guesses. Think of 'vehicle' as a characteristic of 'transportation.'

ex) #1 task type, #2 tools, #3 coworkers, and #4 location

3. List variations of each characteristic. In other words, come up with different words that could be considered part of the characteristic at hand. Stick to less than 20 variations per characteristic. This is best done as a table, hand-drawn or software assisted. Think of variations as 'speed,' 'size,' '# of passengers,' and 'color' as it applies to the characteristic 'vehicle.'

ex) #1 task type: giving status, typing, calculating, speaking, meeting, talking, reading email, making charts, calling

#2 tools: paper, email, text file, Word document, white board, instant message, phone, computer

#3 coworkers: intern, boss, lead, receptionist, administrative assistant, facility representative, cube-mate, senior expert

#4 location: your cube, break room, conference room, at home, in the parking lot, in the lobby, your boss' office

An Example of an Idea Grid Table

Task Type	Tools	Coworkers	Location
giving status	paper	intern	your cube
typing	email	boss	break room
calculating	text file	lead	conference room
speaking	Word document	receptionist	at home
meeting	white board	administration assistant	in the parking lot
talking	instant message	facility representative	in the lobby
reading email	phone	cube-mate	your boss' offoce
making charts	computer	senior expert	
calling			

4. Pick some random combinations or paths through the idea grid and list the results. In other words, randomly pick 1 of the variations of characteristic #1, then randomly pick 1 variation from characteristic #2, and so on until you have 1 variation from each characteristic.

Now make a sentence out of your picks that makes some kind of sense. You don't have to use each variation if it doesn't make sense. You can also change the word order around, as needed.

ex) (a) Reset your motivation by stopping *reading your email*, picking up the *phone*, and asking the *intern* to come to *your cube* to discuss what it will take to tackle important topics.

(b) Get motivation through the ideas of others by *talking* with the *facility representative* in the *lobby* about reducing paper usage in *meetings*.

(c) *Instant message* your group *lead* about facilities to *make charts* in the *break room* to maintain motivation.

(d) *Speak* with your *administrative assistant* in *your cube* about motivation using the *white board* for examples.

~~~

See? Not a tough way to come up with some pretty basic but useful ideas to focus on. Sure, you have to massage them a bit to get something meaningful, but that's part of the process. The key is to get your mind thinking about all of the different combinations you can use to create fresh new content. A cheat-sheet for the Idea Grid method is on the **book resources page**.

Ninja Tip: You can do this table in Excel, use a fancy set of INDEX() and RANDBETWEEN() calls, and create random combinations automatically. I recommend doing it by hand for ultimate creativity, but have included a guiding formula below as a hint.

=INDEX(A:A,RANDBETWEEN(1,COUNTA(A:A)))

Put the formula off in column G. Here your characteristic #1 variations are in column A (without a column heading). Simply repeat this formula for characteristic #2 variations, characteristic #3 variations, and so on and concatenate the answers together. Okay, I'm done with this nerdiness.

Want to really bust your mind around and find some hidden nuggets of awesome? Let's jump into QLQ.

Quantum Linguistic Questioning (QLQ)

This method of brainstorming is useful for thinking about your given situation or topic in ways that are counterintuitive. Yes, you are purposefully trying to wrack your brain so the best stuff floats up to the top. It's tough, but it's a great line of thinking to add to your tool box. It's also an interesting tactic to include in your business ventures. No time to cover business ventures here.

The brain seems to work best, and more fluently, when answering questions, especially questions you've never considered before. The QLQ brainstorming method gets you to turn your main topic into 4 different types of questions designed to get you to consider all angles of the topic.

You can answer all 4 types of questions or just skip to the *Converse* or *Non-Mirror Reverse Question* forms as they tend to REALLY get your mind spinning faster than the others. Here goes:

QLQ Steps:

1. Define your topic in a statement format.

ex) We throw away too much trash.

2. Convert that statement into the Theorem Question form. This is where you turn your topic statement from #1 into a question by adding "what WOULD happen if you DID..." up front:

ex) What WOULD happen if we DID throw away too much trash?

3. Answer the question in as many ways possible. Aim for at least 3 to 5 decent answers.

ex) (1) we would have gigantic piles of junk everywhere
(2) the whole place would begin to stink
(3) tree-hugging hippies (or is it hipsters now?) would start to complain louder
(4) we would be in the habit of wasting as opposed to efficiency
(5) garbage collection companies would be over-burdened and fees would be astronomical

4. Go back and convert your topic statement into the Inverse Question form. This is where you ask "what WOULD happen if you DID NOT?"

ex) What WOULD happen if we DIDN'T throw away too much trash?

5. Now answer the question in as many ways possible. Again, aim for 3 to 5.

ex) (1) garbage companies would have to reduce staff due to low need
(2) landfills could be better utilized for other purposes
(3) trash bag companies would have to diversify income streams or face downsizing
(4) husbands and children alike would have to find additional chores to make up for the void in responsibilities
(5) garbage trucks and workers could do other, non-trash related tasks to supplement the low workload.

6. Convert your topic statement into the Converse Question form. This is you now asking "what WOULD NOT happen if you DID?"

ex) What WOULDN'T happen if we DID throw away too much trash?

7. Answer the question in as many ways possible. 3-5 here, too.

ex) (1) kids wouldn't learn about being more efficient in their product usage
(2) small woodland creatures wouldn't eventually be overrun with piles of smelly garbage
(3) people wouldn't ignore the problem for too long as the pile would eventually block the sun
(4) garbage companies would not have the incentive to streamline their processes
(5) government legislation wouldn't be silent about the ever growing issue of trash.

8. Lastly, convert your topic statement into the Non-Mirror Image Reverse (NMIR) question form. This is where you ask, "what WOULD NOT happen if you DID NOT?"

ex) What WOULDN'T happen if we DIDN'T throw away too much trash?

9. Answer the question in as many ways possible. Aim for 3 to 5. *Warning:* this one is tough but usually provides awesome insights. Don't look to my answers here to convince you, but trust me - this one's a gold-nugget-miner.

ex) (1) people wouldn't be angrily trying to get their neighbors to cut down on their trash creation
(2) manufacturer's would finally stop trying to take care of the problem from their end by creating better packaging
(3) animals wouldn't rebel against humans for attempting to ruin their homelands
(4) people wouldn't increase the understanding of just how important waste-generation awareness is
(5) formal education programs wouldn't begin adding "responsible use planning and engineering" into their curriculum.

~~~

Does your brain hurt, yet? It should and I know mine does. You'll squeeze some great stuff out of there that should yield at least 1 to 3 really decent ideas to focus on. For instance, why the heck aren't colleges creating "responsible use engineering" plans and why aren't more manufacturers taking care of issues from their side? Hmmmm.

Here's a brief summary of the 4 question types to help out for later use.

QLQ Structure:

1) Theorem: WOULD + DID
2) Inverse: WOULD + DID NOT
3) Converse: WOULD NOT + DID
4) NMIR: WOULD NOT + DID NOT

A cheat-sheet for this method is on the **book resources page**, too.

Remember when I said there were some software aided techniques that are out there? Here's one of my most favorite methods. I'll cover the slow but free method first and then dip into the blazingly fast but minimal-cost method second.

Google Prediction Hints

Do something with me here. Open up your browser and go to Google.com. Still have your choice topic in mind? Great. Now type it into the Google search bar. If you have "Google Instant Predictions" enabled, then you will see Google try and guess what you're typing as you type. That's the auto-complete or prediction tool at work.

If it's not coming up, then press the little gear icon in the top-right corner of the Google homepage to access your "Search Settings." Once on the settings page, select "Always show instant results," click the save button, and try again in the Google search bar.

For instance, as I type "stay motivated at " I get the following suggestions or predictions. Quick note, the space in the search term is important as it shows you are looking for another word, which Google is trying to predict:

- work
- the gym
- school
- college
- winter
- sales
- life
- job search
- business
- negative work environment

Hmmmm. Looks like we can talk about staying motivated for a bunch of different markets, places, and audiences. The key to take away from this is you "instantly" have another 10 ideas to talk about staying motivated. But let's take it a bit further since we want to focus on the corporate cube-dweller.

This time, I type in "stay motivated at work " and get the following hints:

- stay motivated at work video
- keeping motivated at work
- can't stay motivated at work
- ways to stay motivated at work
- how to stay motivated at work tips
- quotes to stay motivated at work
- how to stay motivated at work while pregnant

There were a few "workout" or exercise related results I left off as they weren't relevant. Regardless, looking at the results it seems as if we have a few ideas right off the bat. You could create a gigantic list of quotes about motivation at work, you can create a top 10 list of tips for staying motivated, or even an exhaustive list of expecting mother forums as an outlet for motivation by companionship.

Why are these predictions good ideas? Google wouldn't show these predictions unless people were already searching for them. There's no definite way to know how *many* people are searching for them, but there are ways to get an idea of the expected market size. Jump into the good old Google Adwords Keyword Tool... oops... I mean the new Google Keyword Planner.

I won't cover the details of the keyword planner as there are 14 billion other sites that do it already. The gist of this Google Predictor results vetting process is to put your results into the Keyword Planner and see which ones bring in the eyeballs (and possibly cashola).

Ninja Tip: Aim for the really low traffic stuff if you're just starting out. I'm talking about the 1-5 hits per day (30 to 150 local monthly search [LMS] volume) search terms. You've got zero chance at the 3,900 LMS terms if you're a newbie. Aim small and work your way up as your traffic and popularity grows. Climb up that dirty long tail until you can swipe at the head.

Even if you don't get any hits for your prediction ideas in the Google Keyword Planner, it stands to reason that since they were Google's predictions they're still viable ideas. Let's just say that at least 50 to 100 people per month are searching for the prediction terms as a guide. Still worthy targets for newbies.

Great work my friend. You now have a simple, free path for getting a small chunk of ideas on the fly. How long did it take you? Probably not too long. Just 10-20 minutes, right? Cool. I do want to note that getting 5 to 10 decent ideas per Google predictor tool is pretty good for a 10 minute exercise.

Finding good traffic terms in the Google Keyword Planner is even a lower percentage on top of that, however. With some patience, you will be able to nail down some useful and proven terms to focus your blog topic around. But let me put something in perspective for you real quick.

What if you could go get 26,000 Google Predictor results, run them through the vetting process, and see what kind of winners you have? See you next year! Seriously, it can eat up some real time especially if you've been blogging about a topic for long enough to have covered many of the sub-topics.

In steps our saving grace: automation tools. I absolutely love these tools to death. They need to put me in their commercials because I actually feel younger just by using them they save me that much time. Sure, I had to pony over a few bucks (it's not as bad as it sounds), but what's that compared to my irreplaceable time and associated value?

Okay I'm not done, yet. Remember the first time you learned about "copy and paste" in Microsoft Word or Excel? Yeah. It's just like that except you don't even have to press the buttons anymore. Win and win some more. Okay, now I'm done.

Let me go through the real quick overview to give you an idea of what's going on.

Software Automation For The Win

You know the Google Predictor Tool you just used? Well a super-charged front end to it (and Amazon, YouTube, and international Google sites) exists and it's called Keyword Researcher (and has a free trial). You simply type in your term in Keyword Researcher (KR) with a wildcard, hit the 'Play' button, and watch the results roll in. Fast as all get out, too.

Okay so you automatically ran your terms through while you were grabbing some coffee and now have 15,000 results. Now what? Time to run them through the vetting process, but not the same way we did it before. It's time to automate!

This time we rely on Market Samurai (which also has a free trial) to do the grunt work. Open Market Samurai (MS), start a new keyword (doesn't matter what you type - pick one), go to "keyword research," click "add keywords," paste in your results from KR, hit the "Analyze Keywords," and come back a little later.

Sort the results in a manner that works best for you, but I suggest a SEO traffic number of at least 1, a phase-to-broad ratio of at least 2, and an SEO competition number of less than 30,000. After you filter, just export out your results and BAAM you have a list of 100-200 topics to work on. Yup, all done with a total time of 30 minutes maximum for reasonable searches.

Like I said, I understand the bootstrap mentality as I still have it *where it works best* and provides the most use. Do this topic research the manual way a few times through and come to your own conclusions.

For reference, the software links are on the Book Resource Page:

BIG WEBSITES, BIG HINTS

Maybe your focus is a bit more products related. Or maybe you just want to know what kind of hobbies people are interested in the most. Well, I have news for you: they've already told you!

The gist of this line of thinking is to look at what data is already out there and is served up on a silver platter for your taking. When you use the vast world of "sanitized big data" in a way that helps you find your topic ideas, then you're working with proven data.

What happens when a store has a "hot products" or "most popular items" list? Do you go there and see if there is anything you would like to buy, too? Or do you instead go there and figure out what people are buying?

What people are buying is what you want to focus on. Not because you're bargain hunting but because you can ask one simple question and an infinite source of ideas opens for you. Want to know that question? Here it is:

Why?

Simple, right? You want to dive into the shoes of the customer, the target market, and the money-bearer to see what's going on inside their minds. Not just any mInd, but the mind of someone that already spent money on the topic at hand.

Almost every website out there has one of these types of "client interest indicators (CII)" readily available for you to use for your research and profit. Let's dive into a few and see what we can find out.

Look to Hot Products

I won't repeat my diatribe from the paragraphs above here. I just want to jump straight in and get you looking at sites in a whole new way - a more idea rich, and maybe even pocket-rich, way. Also, I visited these sites in mid-August 2013 and they might have changed up a bit. This doesn't affect the point here at all.

www.buy.com (www.rakuten.com)

Just a quick note, buy.com is now officially http://www.rakuten.com/, but buy.com is a whole heck of a lot easier to type.

Head over to buy.com now and look at it with me. I'm not including images here as I really do want you to jump over there and get a feel for it right now. What do you see right away? Here are a couple of things that immediately come to mind for me:

(1) *6 gigantic boxes with featured products* and product groups right below the main sliding advertisements. 2 of these have sale prices included and lead directly to product pages. Are you working on your tech or home & garden blog? Do a review on these hot products or a list of similar items and accompanying comparisons.

(2) *A "Back to School" banner*. Great! No matter what niche you're in, there is something that's relevant to kids, parents, or grandparents that deals with a back to school issue. Sure, this is a seasonal issue, but it's a topic that gets a lot of attention and is important.

(3) *"What's Shakin':* Products with the highest change in sales rank over the past 24 hours" - Hello! This is an especially awesome gold-mine if you're in a product oriented niche and are looking for the latest, greatest, and most popular items to talk about.

There's more, but let's move on to another site so you don't think this was a fluke.

www.overstock.com

(1) *"Overstock has partnered with Snoop" banner*. Oh now if that doesn't have you curious I don't know what will. This is Snoop Lion, by the way, as the Doggy Dogg has been retired. Regardless, product ideas are covered, celebrity hobbyists are covered, and "life changes" or self-help folks are covered. Plenty of topics to gain from that one little banner.

(2) *"As seen in" slider images*. A ton of very popular magazines are listed and have something to do with overstock.com. What markets are targeted? Why would they be interested in the hot products? What are the biggest needs, wants, and fears of that market? What are the article headlines on the magazine covers?

(3) *Compuware best of the web award banner.* This little image is at the bottom of the page. What's it about? What does it take to win? What sites are eligible? Why is this such a brag-worthy feature? Is this something you can do at your own website? What are the biggest web award sites in your niche? Should you be working with them?

Ready for one more? It's still product focused but it's a whole different beast all together.

www.alibaba.com

(1) *Expo-center banner.* This big image is enticing me to play in the "season for innovation" so I must click it. I click over and see a new-fangled, color-changing LED light bulb. Where has lighting technology gone over the last few years? Where do you see it going in the future? How could a revolution in items that are commonly taken for granted change the world for the better?

(2) *Featured partners banner images.* What do these companies do and how do they add value to the world? Why does alibab.com think they are important enough to be featured? Should recommended companies be advertised based on money or contributions alone? What's it like to be a global source of products?

(3) *Industry channel link at the very bottom*. Several hundred links to the biggest, best, and most important industry categories according to alibaba. What's important in "Sports Safety," Agriculture Machinery," or "Skin Care Tools?" How could diving further into the most important products for your industry help you understand the client better?

I think you get the drift when it comes to big product companies and their associated, data-driven, and often very telling promotional design items. Look closely and think deeply. Let's move on to another big source of big ideas.

Only the Biggest Categories

Okay, now you have a grasp on using the biggest and best product focused ways of finding hints at good content ideas. But let's take it up a level or two and broaden our horizons, shall we?

Now you're going to focus on the categories of products, services, and topics that are out there. By seeing how these hints are distributed across different classifications, you can begin to understand the market needs, size, and hunger.

What better way to size up your target market than going and seeing exactly what they're looking for? At the end of the day, the companies doing the selling have the same dilemma as you to address. How do they help clients find what they need in the easiest and most sensible way?

They have to put the products and services where they are best found, best fit, and sell best. They did all the hard work of screening, sifting, and sorting for you. How nice of them, right? Let's see what's here for you.

amazon.com

Head over to amazon.com and get your clicking finger ready for some digging. Now I know Amazon changes their design around a bit from time to time (and they constantly split-test stuff, too) so don't be alarmed if the directions are a little off here. Follow the trail with me.

Click the "Shop By Department" button, choose "Books," and then choose "Kindle Books." Look to the "Categories" section on the left menu down a little ways. Now click the "Nonfiction" link.

Notice something different on the left menu now? Under the "Nonfiction" category are quite a few more subcategories with numbers in parenthesis next to them. The numbers represent the number of books that fall under that category. Now it's just a matter of figuring out what this means to you for finding topics.

There are two main ways to view these numbers:
(1) subcategories with the most books are popular due to *buyer* interest
(2) subcategories with the most books are popular due to *author* interest

Which one do you think matters most for what you're going for? Buyer interest, of course. You want to dive deeper into the categories but with the mind of a buyer.

For instance, while "Nonfiction > Arts & Photography" has 126,619 books, if we follow the most popular deeper subcategories we arrive at "Nonfiction > Arts & Photography > Music > Musical Genres > Classical" with 997 of the total results.

The #1 result in this entire category has a sales rank of #64,373, indicating it sells between 1-3 books per day on average. At about $10, after Amazon's 30% and delivery fees, is a little less than $7 in the author's pocket per book.

That means the author wrote a 192 page book and is making from $7 to $21 from it per day by being the *most popular book* in the subcategory with the *most books* of one of the *main categories* with the *most books*. I'm not saying this is a bad addition to that author's income, but that's a lot of work the get to #1.

On the other hand, when we drill down another huge main category, "Business & Investing," the "Skills" subcategory only has a little over 3,000 titles. However, almost all other subcategories in the "Business & Investing" category have 5 digit title numbers at a minimum, which is at least 3 times more than those in "Skills."

The #1 book in the "Skills > Meetings & Presentations" subcategory has a sales rank of about 4,000 and sells roughly 33 books per day at the same $7 take-home. That's about $7,000 take-home pay per month instead of the roughly $420 on average per month of the "Classical" book before. One is $84,000 per year while the other is $5,040 per year. Forever.

Let's not get bogged down into the numbers much further. My point here is that you will spend the same amount of time creating an awesome piece of content and the same amount of effort to get people to read it. These sales rank numbers are indicators of market needs not author wants. Aim for the market with a *buyer* need so you will be rewarded for your hard work.

Okay back to the idea-generating method at hand.

You can drill through the categories to actually get an idea of what people are looking for and what niche it belongs to. Let's step away from books for a moment, though there are a ton of ideas waiting to be gathered from that section of the Amazon mega-store.

Okay, let's pretend you're a blogger focusing on childhood development and parenting tips. Let's hit the "Toys, Kids, & Baby > Toys & Games" department. Just looking at the categories alone gives you a dozen or more templates to focus your ideas.

For instance, you can directly tackle an article about any of the listings under the "Featured Characters & Brands" heading. These are major characters and brands you now have proof that children are interested in. Amazon doesn't give this kind of premium space to the product-losers when it comes to sales and interest.

Or what about the "Interests > Occupation" category. When you click over to it, you immediately see these are the most popular "what I want to be when I grow up" topics to talk about. I'm seeing Astronaut, Ballerina, Chef, Circus Performer, Construction Worker, Cowboy & Cowgirl, Doctor, Farmer, Firefighter, Military, Nurse, Pirate, Police, and Spy. Could you write something fun about any of those?

Yes, I chose a silly category path to follow, but I did that on purpose. I want to make it clear that Amazon has done a *ton* of work to clearly organize the information their customers need to find. Leverage Amazon's hard work to your advantage and you will be talking directly to the biggest and hungriest audiences, by design.

Ninja-tip: Look at the comments for the "Best Sellers" in your niche of choice. Drill down to the 2 star and 4 star reviews. The customers are telling you exactly what they experienced, what they liked, what they didn't like, and what they'd like to see in future versions. Each comment is a separate topic for your idea-generation-machine. Get to cracking!

After that rather lengthy disclaimer to the Amazon approach, I think we can dive right into the eBay category method and do quite well. Get ready to have more ideas than you'll ever know what to do with.

ebay.com

Navigate to ebay.com, click the "Shop by Category" link next to the eBay logo, and then choose "See All Categories" in the bottom right of the popup menu. A page with a gazillion categories shows up. This page alone is golden as it breaks down ideas into concrete groups, but we're not stopping there.

Scroll all the way to the very bottom of the page. You should see a "Show item counts" link down there. Click it. The page it takes you to should just about blow your mind. In addition to there being a boat-load of deeper categories, there are popular subcategories for each, and they all have the total items currently under auction next to each one.

But it doesn't even stop there. Under each main category is a "See all..." link. Simply find the niche you are interested in, click the "See all..." link for that niche, and go to the resultant deeper subcategorized page of information.

I drilled down into the "Pet Supplies" category and see tons of listings for "Dog Lover Products," "Filter Media & Accessories," "Flea & Tick Remedies," and "Bite Sleeves & Bite Suits." A pet owner article writer or researcher could probably get quite a bit of information from these trails of ideas.

Ninja Tip: If you're into making niche affiliate or AdSense sites, welcome to the wild world of undiscovered products to target here. That is all.

Let's jump into a method that is a little more direct and requires less thinking about products.

Frequently Asked Questions, Answered

Have you ever given a good bit of thought to what a Frequently Asked Question (FAQ) section on a big corporate website is really doing? I mean, why would a company want to put up a page specifically for questions and answers?

It's simple and obvious, but I don't think most people have thought about it from an idea-generation perspective. Let's flip it on its side and look at it real good. An FAQ is a listing of the most common, time-consuming, and easily handled issues that a company has to deal with on a regular basis. In a word: popular.

An FAQ is a goldmine of topics, hints, and clues to subjects you should also address in your own business or hobby ventures. If you know of a large corporation in your niche, chances are you can write an article or 10 on every one of the FAQ's they have listed.

Let's look at Geico for a moment. Head over to Google and search for the following:

+"life insurance" +FAQ

After the results pop up, scroll down a bit to hit Geico's entry. Once you're on Geico's life insurance FAQ page you'll see the following FAQ's listed:

- Why do I need life insurance?
- How do I know how much life insurance I need?
- Who should I buy life insurance from?
- What are the advantages of term life insurance?
- Can I afford term life insurance?
- What should I look for in a term life policy?
- How do I decide the number of years (term) to choose for my policy?
- How often should I review my life insurance needs?
- What coverages does term life provide?
- Who can I name as beneficiaries?

Could your insurance or financial wellness website do anything with those ideas? Heck, those look like straight-up blog post headlines to me. Want to know the best part of this method? If you're looking for a refresher on the topic, just read the answer to the FAQ! Bingo-bango, done and done.

You can find relevant FAQ's for your niche by repeating the Google search you did for Geico but by switching out the "life insurance" for "YOUR NICHE." I suggest hitting up as many as you can In a row and just create a gigantic bank of topics to address. You'll be covered for months to come.

Lastly, let's look through an often quoted method that is just as often not explained well enough.

Forums That Matter

How do you get inside of your clients', readers', and prospects' heads? You either ask them or read their personal insights already voluntarily spread out all over the internet. The latter option is so much easier and cheaper to implement. Go to the niche specific forums.

No, I am not going to stop there and just send you off with that very vague advice. Let's dip our toes into this wonderfully telling method of generating a plethora of awesome ideas. I'm going to dip into the "self-help" and "self-esteem" topic here for that large blogging audience.

We're going to look for relevant topics on helping people gain confidence, growing emotionally, and working toward a more successful future. Go over to Google and run the following search query.

+confidence +forums

A few results down I chose the "http://www.depressionforums.org/" entry. I ignored the post it took me to and looked directly for the "breadcrumb structure" or navigation trail at the top" For instance, it showed I was in the "The Depression Forums - A Depression & Mental Health Social Community Support Group > DEPRESSION RELATED FORUMS > DEPRESSION CENTRAL" section.

I then clicked the "Depression Central" link in that breadcrumb menu. That brings me to a listing of all posts in that section. This isn't always the case, but this forum was nice enough to include a "most viewed" and "most replied" sorting option.

Sorting by "most viewed" lists up top the forum thread titled "Answers To Curing Anhedonia/numbness/zombieness/no Emotions/apathy/no Libido. Collective Experiences" with 1,887 replies and 142,596 views. That is a *ton* of eyes and a book's worth of replies. Do you think there's a topic hidden in there or not?

Oh by the way, there were 461 more pages of 25 or more threads per page in that one specific forum. That website also has 47 other forums full of topics, highly-motivated users, and wonderfully useful topics to talk about. You know what the best part is? You'll be talking about things that really do help people.

Switch over to your niche and look for the most obviously sought after topics. You'll quickly find yourself smack in the middle of topics people are looking to read. Plus, you'll know which answers helped the forum posters the most and which ones were proven to be bunk. Win for them and win for you.

Unlimited Ideas In Your List

I know most people aren't sure how to pick idea topics that have been proven to be useful and relevant. Anyone can brainstorm an idea from scratch, but most people stop there as they tend to freeze up from not knowing whether their ideas are "good enough."

You don't need to worry about that anymore.

Let me tell you that you are now equipped with some very powerful tools to not only have an unlimited flow of ideas but to also judge how effective and relevant they are to your target audience.

Here's a recap of the methods you can use:

(1) Look to Hot Products
(2) Only the Biggest Categories
(3) Frequently Asked Questions, Answered
(4) Forums That Matter

Learn to leverage the hard work of others and you'll instantly multiply your efforts. It's been said your best bet is to use the resources that are in abundance to make up for those that are lacking. Use the crowd-sourced idea-generation of others to make up for the lack of writing topics.

Now what about your competition? What are they up to? Surely they've got some awesome ideas you can learn from, right?

LEARN FROM THE COMPETITION

When it comes to finding ideas to go over, you want to focus on what's interesting, proven useful for your target audience, and worth your time. Why reinvent the wheel? Let's just go look at what's working very well for your competition and base your efforts off of their hard research.

Okay, okay, don't get all upset as I am not suggesting you copy anything.

But I am suggesting you go to those who've done it before to see what's working for them. If you want to get into the restaurant business, then are you going to try some brand new dish or a variation of what's popular for your area? Hamburgers and chicken fingers for the kiddos, fajitas and chicken fried steak for the adults is a great start. You can optimize later.

Finding The Competition

You've probably never purposefully looked for a website that helps you find sites that are similar to what you're looking for. After all, why would you as this is a pretty specific need, unless you're doing the research you'll be doing soon.

If you know of a competitor right off the bat, then you're golden. If you need some help, then use Google to search for the general idea of what your biggest competitor actually does. Take those top 3 to 5 results and record the links (URLs) down into a plain text file or spreadsheet.

For instance, if you're looking for ideas on how to make money while blogging, then type in "how to make money blogging." Simple, right? **Problogger** and **Copyblogger** show up towards the top and are absolutely great sources of good ideas. They're also great sites in general.

As a side note, when I say "biggest competitor" I mean either literally the most popular website in your niche or simply a provider of content on the topic you're targeting. If you're not sure of the topic you want to target, then it might be time to review the brainstorming section again.

Now go to the following "similar site" searching websites, paste in the URLs you copied previously, and start digging around:

http://www.similarsitesearch.com/
http://www.similarsites.com/

I always have cleaner and better results with the first link, but both are decent sources.

As an example of what you get, when I type in "richardstep.com" in the first link's search tool, I get the following sites that are deemed "similar to" my own site:

http://www.humanmetrics.com/
http://www.keirsey.com/
http://www.stevepavlina.com/
http://similarminds.com/

Yes, there were a few irrelevant matches, but for the most part a quick view of the resulting websites will tell you if they are similar enough for your purposes or not. The key here is to find sites that are doing it and doing it well.

Now, I would take any of the 4 sites I found and begin the researching process, which we'll get to in just a second.

Alternatives to Similar Site Searches

If you don't seem to be getting any decent results from the similar sites search method, then you can rest your trust in Google for some decent results. Take the main topic you have in mind or that your biggest competitor claims to be good at. Look to their tagline, navigation menu links, and any categories they chose to make the most obvious.

As an example, when I click over to SimilarMinds site, I see a link to "Personality Types." When I drill a bit further, I end up on the INTJ page for the Jungian Personality Types, which is highly relevant to my personal and career development audience. This is something for me to talk about.

Once you get a feel for what the competition is focusing profitably on, then head over to Google and search for that exact topic in quotation marks. Google will give you what it believes are the best results for that topic.

Look to the first 10 results, capture their URL's, and add them to your "to research" list. Pay attention to the ads that pop up on the Google results page, too. Those are usually companies or websites that have money to spend, which can be a good indicator of success.

Begin the Research Process

It's time to dive right into figuring out what's been working best for everyone else in your space. Put your detective hat on, but not too tight as this is some pretty easy stuff.

Pick any of your "competitor" or "similar site" websites and begin to dig in using the following ideas. Record your notes into a spreadsheet so you can sift, sort, and screen as you go along and get stuff done. We'll call this the "Winner-Sheet" or WS.

What To Look For

With the wonderful social revolution comes the interest in sharing anything and everything with the world. While there are some nightmare examples of this going wrong, we're going to focus on the good stuff here to get you what you need.

Look to comments, tweets, and social sharing numbers for hints of the really popular stuff. As you look around, you'll find widgets or special features that brag about "the most commented posts" or "most popular commenter." These widgets or content areas usually list the top 5-10 posts that are getting the most love from viewers. This is a good thing. Take note of the most commented posts and add them to your WS.

How about views? Are the views made public for the site you're at? If so, then repeat the process for high-view count posts. This is especially useful for the "forums" section, if it exists. Again, most websites owners are proud of their popular posts and will put popular posts (or a widget thereby) telling you exactly what you need to know. Add them to your WS.

Lastly, check the navigation menu, footer area, and sidebars for the links the website owner thinks you should pay attention to. Chances are, they are trying to get you to click on things that are working best for them. Similarly, these are the exact things you need to add to your WS.

And If You're Super Lucky...

Some sites, in the interest of showing their viewers just how awesome they are at providing good content, will put it all on a silver platter for you. Simply go to their "blog" or "archives" section and look for a complete listing of all posts done to date.

For instance, Pick The Brain (great site, by the way) has an articles section that has an "archives" sub-section.

http://www.pickthebrain.com/blog/archives-new/

After you press the "expand all" link, every single post they've done since 2006 comes flooding over your screen. Now you can open up each link that interests you, check for social signals or comments proving it is popular, and save that URL in your WS.

...or you can bulk it up and be a complete ninja... hang tight for a second for that tip.

Before we get into it, I know Google's PageRank (PR) factor is only 1 of over 200 ranking factors when it comes to showing up in search engines. And I don't care as that's not the point here. What you're going to do here is capture as many URLs from the website's archive list and do a "bulk PR check" on them to get a *hint* of their success.

I just grabbed a handful of links from PickTheBrain's list, Googled "bulk PR check", picked one of the PR-checking sites that showed up, and went to town. After a few seconds, the PR for every link was displayed on my screen. Out of the 7 links I tested, 2 were PR0 (meh), 3 were PR2 (okay), and 2 were PR3 (not bad).

The higher the PR, the better. As PR is an *indicator* of popularity over time, it stands to reason that the higher PR links are a decent topic for you to cover. Add them to your WS and let's move on.

Ninja Tip: Want to copy ALL links on a complete archives list? You can either look to a link-scraper tool (I won't recommend any, sorry) or look to the source. Go to the page, view the source code, and copy the main link section. Paste the results into a text editor like the free **Notepad++** and then clean up the links. Piece of cake.

Now let's jump into what to do with these popular links you're been putting in your Winner-Sheet.

What To Get From It All

Time to dive into the list of links on your WS and see what you can come up with. As a guiding principle, your overall goal is to "meta" your competition's approach and to *not* copy anything. Let me reiterate: DO NOT copy the stuff you are finding.

What do I mean by "meta" their approach? Simple. Look to the ideas, guiding principles, or topics that led them to create the content they did. For example, the "how lazy couch potatoes can lose weight without exercise" post is simply the "weight loss" topic targeted at folks who don't enjoy exercising at all.

Look to the 3-5 word "guiding topic" that is a "level above" what the sites are creating.

In other words, when you look at McDonald's for restaurant ideas, don't call your restaurant McDowel's and stock the Big Matt hamburger. Create your burger joint, call it something relevant to your audience, and fill it with burgers *based* on winning models but tailored to your personality and audience interests.

Make what you find into something that is uniquely you and relevant to those who you are targeting. Yes, you can find the "how to stay motivated at school" topic and turn it around to the "be eternally motivated at work" topic. Take their "idea seeds" and turn them into your own fruitful trees.

That's basically the gist of the method here. Let me recap it to make it stick:

1) Find sites that are rocking it
2) Find what's working for them
3) Figure out what the popular stuff is about
4) Use those ideas as your content seeds
5) Create new, uniquely you content

And remember, stay calm and do not copy. It's time to put all of these ideas you've compiled in your Winner-Sheet into the real world. It's time to implement and execute. Carry on and let's bring some good ideas to life.

PART 2

CONTENT CREATION MACHINE

LEARN TO TEACH, DICTATE ACTIONS LATER

You've been thinking about the QCF for a while now, having made it this far. You probably had no idea you would be so good at finding ideas, but you're there. You know you're going to dive into dictation and become well versed. But doesn't it seem like there's a piece missing?

How they heck do you know if what you're dictating will make any sense?

Much like learning how to throw a ball doesn't mean you'll be an all-star baseball pitcher, just learning the mechanics of dictating will not make you an *effective* content generation and delivery guru.

Before you jump right into learning how to record the thoughts coming out of your mouth, let's make sure they're coming out the right way. Let's build up your ability to teach the way people like to learn, and then we can jump into dictating like crazy.

It's All About The 4MAT, Baby

You've no doubt sat in a class before, were bored to death, and didn't end up learning much from it, right? All that time wasted and you wanted to be anywhere but there. Sure, some classes were better, but I bet it was because of the teacher. There's good reason for this, too.

The last thing we want to do is try to teach, educate, and write in a way that bores readers to death. We want to grab attention, inform, motivate, and encourage continual forward motion. We want people to be engaged and to take action. We want to speak to people in the way that works best for their learning preference and personality.

In 1972, Bernice McCarthy developed the 4MAT System to help teachers better form their curriculum based on the different ways people learn. This system uses the known differences in learning styles and brain-dominance preferences (left or right, logical or free-form) to pick the "path of least resistance" for getting the information to stick.

Deep down you know your readers are not just like you, but you tend to write the only way you know how: the way you like it! However, there are 4 major learning styles we need to talk to:

4 Major Learning Styles:

1) Imaginative Learners
2) Analytic Learners
3) Common Sense Learners
4) Dynamic Learners

I won't get any further into the details here, but let's just say we have a few steps to go through (and in the correct order) before we can speak well to all interested learning styles.

Bernice's research leads to an 8 step process that covers the left and right brained approach to all 4 learning styles. However, that's just too much work for practical and quick content.

That's why I'm breaking it down into 4 main steps:

1) Tell them 'what'
2) Tell them 'why'
3) Tell them 'how'
4) Tell them 'what if' or 'what now'

This might look familiar to you if you've ever read up on copywriting. The AIDA (attention/awareness, interest, decision/desire, action) principles are based off of this same line of brain-based learning, though AIDA was formulated much earlier than 4MAT.

Remember this forever: people need to know what's in it for them, how they'll benefit, what steps it'll take, and how to bring it all to life. Why reinvent the wheel for your content?

Let me break down these 4 steps into a bit more detail to help show what I mean. Keep this information in mind because it'll be the basis of how you dictate your content later. It also gets pretty easy once you get the flow down.

Note: each step has a "Bring it to life" list at the end. These are guidelines to direct your dictation. It's not important for you to memorize them here, but due plant those seeds and let them grow now.

Step 1) Tell Them 'What'

This can be a cut and dry summary of what you are about to tell them or you can make it mean more. The world loves story-telling and it has been an effective method of teaching-with-interest since time began. I encourage you to tie the "what" to something a little less direct or rote.

In other words, while it'll work, I don't recommend reading the verbatim definition of "global thermonuclear war." Instead, start your dictation off with how you felt the first time you saw David (Broderick) take on Joshua (WOPR) in War Games (1983). Okay so it's an old movie and I was only 4 years old at the time, but if you've seen it you had an emotional response from the scene.

That's the ultimate goal of what you're going for here. First, you want to let them know what they are learning about because the brain just doesn't give a hoot if it isn't directed to focus on something concrete. Second, tying what you're teaching to something emotional, personal, or impactful to make it all that much stickier.

Use a personal story if you can that way they'll learn to know you, like you, and trust you along the way. However, referencing news articles, pop culture, or hypothetical situations works just fine, too. Remember: tell them 'what' and make it interesting.

Bringing it to Life:
- aim for 3 to 5 sentences max
- take no more than 45 seconds

Step 2) Tell Them 'Why'

What would you say if someone came right up to you, put their hand in front of your face, and asked you to say the alphabet with your eyes closed? Okay, my first reaction would probably be to dismiss such a weird person, but my next action might be to blurt out a big "why?"

If you're looking to capture the hearts, minds, and attention of others, then you'll need to let them know *why* the hee-haw they should even be paying attention to you. On top of that, they'll need to know what they will get out of it. You know, the proverbial "what's in it for me?"

Use this brief section to let your readers or viewers know why they should even care about what you're saying. Skip this step and the brain is constantly telling its owner, "this is not important enough to listen to." Put that brain at ease and give it what it wants: tell it why it should listen.

Bringing it to Life:
- aim for 2-3 sentences
- take no more than 30 seconds

Step 3) Tell Them 'How'

This is the meat and potatoes of the presentation, post, article, or email. You'll jump straight into the main points that make up the "how to" or "most important steps" for accomplishing what you're setting out to teach them.

If the content is about washing a car, then this section will include sections that cover materials needed, special techniques, the washing routine, the rinsing plan, and the drying method. Break down whatever it is you're talking about into 3 to 7 main points at most.

I have a word of caution though. To meet the 5-minute time frame you're working with, you have no more than 3 minutes and 15 seconds (3.25 minutes) for this section. That means if you pick 3 main points, you have 3.25/3 minutes to discuss each one (or 1 minute and 5 seconds each). This means that content with 7 points will only have 3.25/7 minutes to discuss each point (or about 28 seconds each).

Keep this "points to minutes" formula in mind as it'll be much tougher to put a ton of useful content into a 28 seconds block of time than it will be for a 1-minute block. Sometimes you just have to pick the best 3 points out of 7 in order to cover the material appropriately. At the end of the day, whatever you produce will be useful and you can always split it into several pieces of content, if needed.

Bringing it to Life:
- length depends on the number of points to discuss
- remember the 3.25 minutes divided by # of points rule
- take no more than 3.25 minutes total

Step 4) Tell Them 'What If and What Now'

Try not to make this section any more complicated that it has to be. This is a straight-up summary or restatement of the main points and the goal the reader is trying to achieve. Follow that up with a one or two sentence blurb about what you want them to do next and then you're done.

You've only got space for about 2-4 sentences here so make them count. Don't worry about getting the call-to-action down pat here as you can always update it and add the right information once you get the transcription back.

Most of the time I don't even do the call-to-action part as I use a script to split test my calls-to-action and will just put the verbiage in that script when I'm done.

Bringing it to Life:
- 2-4 sentences max
- take no more than 30 seconds

Ninja Tip: When you're looking to convince others to do something (especially toddlers and kindergartners!), start talking to them in this "what, why, how, what now" 4 step way. Give them a real brief idea of what you're talking about, tell them why it's important *to them*, give the couple of steps you want done, and then get them going.

Creating Cue Cards

The 4 step-related sections you just read are full of way more detail than you want to think about when you're actually doing the dictation. You will need some form of dictation guide to help channel your creative juices in the direction you need them to go. It's time to create a template for guiding your train of thoughts so you don't derail and ramble on for the whole 5 minutes.

This really is as simple and straight-forward as you want it to be. I recommend using index cards for the first couple of rounds and then going to a digital solution shortly thereafter. I'll go through the general format of what the cue card needs to contain regardless of how you bring it to life.

There are only a few things you need to include on the card itself and you want to limit the space you have to write. Limiting your space ensures you are not reading straight off the card and are simply cuing yourself along the 4MAT path of teaching effectively. And it's dang simple to do.

Cue Card Contents:

Line 1: Your punchy headline - make it as bland or "magazine headline" quality as you like. I recommend making it sensational as it sets the mood for the rest of the dictation.

Line 2: leave it blank

Line 3: write "what?" and then a 5-10 word reminder of the main subject. I like to make this a few words that remind me of the story I want to tie the content to.

Line 4: write "why?" and then a 5-10 word reminder of "what's in it for them?"

Line 5: write "1)" and then a 5 to 10 word reminder of the 1st main point

Line 6 through 11: repeat the line 5 step for as many points as you have

PowerPoint Cue Card Example:

~~~

That's it! I highly recommend you scribble the date or category of the topic you're dictating about in one of the corners. This will help you sort and organize your cards for later.

After you've tried the index card method a few times, it's probably time to kick it up a notch and stop yourself from having to carry around 3"x5" paper where ever you go.

Simply create the cue card in Microsoft PowerPoint, save the slide as a PNG (available in the "File > Save As" menu), and then put the image on your smart-phone. You now have your cue cards ready to go any time you want.

Ninja Tip: Your phone's battery probably won't last forever. If you aren't able to have it plugged in while you dictate, consider using black background & white text slides to help minimize power usage by the screen. It may be a minimal savings, but that might be the minute or two you need at the end of a recording.

Okay - I think that's just about enough of the nitty-gritty information on this method of dictation planning. Now it's time to learn about bringing these awesome posts, articles, and emails to life.

TIME TO EXECUTE YOUR IDEAS

You've probably heard this saying before. It goes something like, "ideas aren't worth much until they're implemented." Well, I'm here to tell you that saying is absolutely correct. You've done a lot of great work up to this point and now's the time to bring that content right out of you.

If you've never dictated anything before, then this might seem a little scary for you at first. Fret not my esteemed content generating master in training. You'll be creating content at break-neck speeds in no time when you go through the plan before you here.

You've done the content preparation and know exactly what you're going to talk about. Now it's just a matter of making sure the external factors are taken care of before you start recording. Then it's time to record great new, unique, and awesome content like I know you can.

To make this part of the process smooth, you've got to get your mind right, choose the right environment, use the right equipment, do the work, and know how to handle mistakes. Simple stuff. Let's get it.

A Quick Note About Dictation Software

I've done it, trained the heck of it for weeks, and I don't like it. Your mileage may vary. Personally, I don't enjoy saying all of the periods, new lines, and punctuation marks. It's so much easier for someone to just put those in there for me.

After all, I am aiming for ultimate speed and the flow really is halted when you have to convince the software you said "new line" instead of "nude lion" - 7 times in a row. Give it a shot if you are interested, but I wouldn't get your hopes up.

Hopefully, one day dictation software will be seamless and wonderfully effective. I don't believe we are there yet. Until that day comes, let's work with the method that is smooth and working great.

Mental Readiness & Confidence

No, dictating is not public speaking and your entire high school class is not watching you. No matter how introverted or shy you think you are, this speaking-gig is about as private as it comes. This is just you recording your own personal thoughts into a machine.

Approach this entire dictation process with an air of confidence. Know that no matter what you say, you can always either delete it, chop it out of the audio file later, or just edit the transcribed text. You have layers upon layers of chances to refine and hone your work. You are in control.

This whole process is simply a very basic and rough draft. All first drafts are going to mostly suck. It's going to be full of stammering, run-on sentences, and malformed thoughts at first. But it gets better. You start to transform your abilities the more you do it. It's really a cool process.

This may sound goofy, but I recommend you get into the routine of psyching yourself up before each recording. You'll want to be about 150% of your normal self while recording. Yes, that means you might sound cheesy, you might feel fake, and you'll probably be uncomfortable at first.

But with time and practice, your content will come alive with the same vigor and positive attitude you get yourself into before you get started. Get your mind right and the rest will just come flowing out. I think you'll be surprised with what you're able to produce after a few rounds.

As a guide, think about how you feel, act, and converse when around friends. Now compare that to how you feel, act, and converse in a business meeting. Big difference, right? Go with the "around friends" version, please.

Steady Your Environment

How often do you notice the kids playing in the street, the birds chirping in the background, or the sound coming from you tapping your pen on the table? Not often, right? There is a ton of background noise that we've come to ignore as it's not relevant to the task at hand.

However, if you're recording yourself speaking for you or someone else to transcribe later, then I firmly believe your audio quality should be pretty dang good. The quality of your audio is normally dependent on two main things: (1) environment and (2) equipment. Know-how fits in there, but that's a given.

Before you start your next recording session, please be sure to calm and form the area around you. Pick a quiet, not-frequently disturbed area of your house or recording area. Let's run through a list of some of the common environmental sound issues that come up:

- neighbors mowing the lawn
- dish washer, washing machine, or the dryer are running
- wearing crunchy or loud clothes
- interference caused by electronics or lights (turn them off)
- cell phones ringing or vibrating
- background TV noise
- smoke alarm "change battery" chirp
- your hands and elbows bumping the stand or table the microphone is on
- fans and air conditioners
- sound reflection or echo off of walls

Basically, you probably need to sit in your proposed recording spot and begin to focus on each sound that stands out. I also encourage you to record some "dead air" for about a minute and listen to it from your computer to get the ultimate idea of audio quality you can achieve. Use headphones, too.

One by one, minimize the sounds that are being picked up by your recorder. You'll eventually be at a place where you get some pretty dog gone good audio no matter how old or non-fancy your equipment might be. *Note:* even fancy-equipment makes bad quality audio if the environment is poorly selected.

One last point here: make sure you will be interrupted as few times as possible. I've got 2 kids and a lovely wife that really do enjoy spending time with me. Sometimes it's especially hard to find some quiet time unless I specifically plan it out. The same may be true for you.

It's *very* tough to carry on in a dictation when someone enters the room during your recording. It gets better with practice, but it really does kick you right out of that "recording state." Do what you can to prepare and inform them ahead of time to avoid this situation.

Equipment Does Matter

Yes, you can get by with just about whatever recording device you want using whichever cue card system works best for you. However, I'd like you to consider a few things first before you use a cheapo headset outside in the wind and go to town on your dictations.

You need to keep the future in mind. I'm not just talking about what you get out of it; I am talking about transcriber experience and leveraged use of every piece of content you ever make. I will cover getting the most out of your work through leveraging in another book as the topic is too broad for this book.

I've done some dictation while using my smart phone's built-in microphone, on the highway, with the tons of road noise all along the way. I thought it sounded absolutely horrible, but the awesome transcribers were able to very accurately lift out the text.

And I felt obligated to pay them double the nominal rate for it, too. It is substantially harder for anyone to transcribe audio when there is a ton of background noise or distractions. More difficult audio means less accurate translations. Just don't do it to yourself or anyone else unless you want to pay for the more difficult work.

Let me run through a couple of my own setups to give you an idea of what works and where.

Smartphone + App

My Android powered smartphone has proved to be a useful tool for a low noise environment. For instance, when I am a quiet area (or in my parked car), I can get a pretty good quality recording. Yes, it is a bit noisy in the background but the quality is almost good enough to repurpose and certainly good enough for transcription.

There's just one catch. Most of the built-in apps don't allow you to control the quality settings of the audio encoding. I use an app called 'ASR' and am able to record in stereo at whatever bitrate I choose. I normally sit at 192 kbps and choose an encoding quality value of 4. The sound is great.

The app is free with adverts and limited support, though I highly recommend buying it as it's a great app and only a few bucks. Here's a Google shortlink to it:

http://goo.gl/Mxnsp5

Ninja Tip: Here's another neat trick. You can pull up ASR, start recording, hit the home button to pop out of it, head over to your Gallery app, pull up your image cue cards, and just start recording right away. Your smartphone becomes your recording device *and* cue card system. Very, very handy and makes recording a blog post anywhere, anytime absolutely doable.

Vocal Booth + Recorder + Phone

A vocal booth + microphone + phone cue card system is my go to setup for recording "studio quality" audio. I go all out when I know I am going to repurpose the audio for video mixing later, audiobooks, or just bonus give-a-ways. There's a huge difference between the phone + app setup and this. Every decibel counts!

To this day, I still use my own finagled together vocal booth. I came across some high quality foam and attached it to a storage crate from the local home goods store. The idea is to put the microphone inside the vocal booth with only one side exposed to your voice. This cuts down on ambient noise from all other directions.

I spent a little extra (but not too much) and use either the Rode Videomic shotgun microphone or the Zoom H2n for the higher quality recordings. Yes, there are much better tools for the job. Yes, they also cost 4-10 times more money, too. For most uses, what I have is very good at doing a bang-up job when the environment is setup correctly.

I do tend to tip my hat to the H2n as it's got an onscreen timer, which is great for pacing your dictation. Sure, I also have a separate kitchen timer for any other recording setups, but the less buttons I have to press the better.

After everything is set up, I then open up the Gallery app on my smartphone and proceed to use the cue card images as my dictation guides. As soon as I finish one dictation, I delete the image and move on to the next task at hand.

Ninja Tip: Don't waste $25 on a smartphone stand or holder for this cue card purpose. Go to your local office supply store and spend $2 on a business card holder. Works great.

When all is said and done, the sound turns out great, the flow is nice, and it feels good. I even receive feedback from my transcribers stating what a pleasure it was to transcribe such high quality audio. Talk about making me feel good - nice bonus!

I've got some links, pictures of my scrappy setup, and other goodies about my hardware choices over on the book resources page - **check it out**.

At the end of the day, whatever you have available is going to work and you should never let the tools stop you from doing what you want to do. A producer produces no matter what and mastering a "less than optimal" setup will only make you that much better when you upgrade.

Now let's get into the details of actually doing to dictation, shall we?

Do The Dictation Already!

I'd like to say this is going to be complex just to make it seem like this is some type of genius process or something. To tell you the truth, you've already done the hard part once you're here. Now it's just time to hit the record button and let it flow.

However, there are a few pointers I'd like to give you to help make it flow as easily as possible. I'm going to jump right into the scenario of you having everything setup and in good order already. Pretend you just hit the record button and are about to begin your dictation. Here's how I suggest you handle it.

Ninja Tip: It's good to work a good, SEO-friendly keyword into the article while you're at it. Make the keyword part of your title and be sure to use it at least one time in the 'what' or 'why' portion of the dictation. Use a variation or closely related term in the ending summary, too.

Dictation Steps:

1) Say the headline with gusto and power

2) Wait 2-3 seconds

3) Do the 'what' part for no more than 45 seconds

4) Do the 'why' part for no more than 30 seconds. Try to work your keyword in here.

5) Jump into Point # 1 and actually start it off by saying "Number 1" with a short pause. This will help organizing the transcription later and cues the transcriber to make distinct paragraphs or sections in the results.

6) Run through the rest of the points using the 3.25 / "# of points" formula as a guide. I've included a chart below to help make the math easy.

7) Say "conclusion"

8) Wait 2-3 seconds

9) Run through your 30 second closing & call-to-action

<center>~~~</center>

See? Not much to it. It'll take some practice to remember to say "conclusion" and speak the numbers out, but more often than not the transcribers catch on and have got your back. It's great teamwork.

Here's the time-chart to help breakdown how much time you have for each main point depending on how many points you have:

Dictation Timing Guide (5 Minutes Max)

	Total # of Points				
	3	**4**	**5**	**6**	**7**
Start	0:00	0:00	0:00	0:00	0:00
Point #1	1:15	1:15	1:15	1:15	1:15
Point #2	2:20	2:04	1:54	1:48	1:43
Point #3	3:25	2:53	2:33	2:21	2:11
Point #4	4:30	3:42	3:12	2:54	2:39
Point #5	-	4:31	3:51	3:27	3:07
Point #6	-	-	4:30	4:00	3:35
Point #7	-	-	-	4:33	4:03
Conclusion	-	-	-	-	4:31
End	5:00	5:00	5:00	5:00	5:00

http://richardstep.com/QCF

What this chart is saying is that if you have 3 points, then you should start point #1 by 1:15 on your timer, start point #2 by 2:20 on your timer, start point #3 by 3:25 on your timer, and be ready to jump into the conclusion by 4:30 on your timer. If you're running late on an early point, then just make up for it a bit later. There's a cheat-sheet for this chart on the **resources page**.

But what about mistakes you ask? No problem. They happen, they can be funny as heck, and you need to learn to work with them. Here's what I've learned along the way.

Make the Most of Mistakes

Let's face it, you won't be fired up, super on-point, or at your very best every single time you dictate a piece of content. That's perfectly fine and something you'll learn to work with. The key is to make life easier and keep on flowing. Don't stop, keep rocking, and produce like crazy.

If you catch yourself making a minor mistake, then just recollect yourself within the second, say what you meant to say, and continue on. You can also specifically direct the transcriber to correct something, but I wouldn't do this often as you're paying for it, literally.

My preferred method of dealing with rather large mistakes is to just beep them out. Yup - with my own voice, too. My wife loves it so much to hear me do this from another room. Over and over and over again.

When you catch yourself at a mistake point, just blurt out a high-pitched 'beep' sound for about 3-5 seconds. You'll be able to easily find this beep section when you edit the file later. This is audio marking for the win.

If all of this seems like it's still too much to pay attention to in the heat of the dictation, then you're not alone. Sometimes you are just in such a flow state you won't even know when a mistake comes rolling by.

Trust the transcriber.

With the proper screening, you'll be working with good transcribers who know the ins and outs of doing this task. They will always err on the side of caution or put a note to you in the transcription. The good ones take their work very seriously.

Also, asking for a *nonverbatim* transcription works wonders. That's like secret code for "make me sound a little better, please."

And there you have it. You've now got a wonderfully dictated piece of content just waiting to be transformed into something everyone can read. Let's get on that, shall we?

LET THERE BE TRANSCRIPTIONS

Ahhh. We finally get to the part where your words come to life. All of the hard work you've done so far comes down to transforming a couple of MP3 or WAV files into your next great piece of content to release out into the world... after some editing, of course.

There are two main approaches to this part of the process you should consider. Do you want to do it yourself for 'free' (time really isn't a free resource), or do you spend a few bucks and get someone else to transcribe your hard work? This can be a real tough decision for most folks to make.

Some Common Cautions to Dismiss

Super-duper boot-strappers probably don't see the value in spending cash for doing something they can do quite easily. Similarly, some won't feel comfortable releasing their content out to the masses for fear or embarrassment or plagiarism. These are all legitimate concerns, but hardly something you should worry about.

In the case of not spending money, I highly recommend you do a few transcriptions yourself first. This is a very valuable experience for both understanding the work involved and also how the process works. We'll go through some self-transcription tips that will help make it easier even though I recommend moving on to paying others to transcribe your work as quickly as you can.

Now if you're worried about embarrassment, forget about it. You'll be amazed at some of the down-right horrible quality (and sometimes horrible content!) that transcribers have to trudge through. If you simply try your best, have decent quality audio, and treat transcribers nicely, then you'll be just fine.

Oh and don't worry about plagiarism. Yes, it *can* happen, but the probability is very low. Remember this; nothing stops someone from coming by your blog and just copying and pasting the content over to their site as it is. Besides, you're going to beef it up, revise it, and make it awesomely you. Trust me, this is something you shouldn't let stop you.

If you're still really worried about plagiarism, then you can chop your audio files into smaller chunks (e.g. 30 seconds per file). This would vastly reduce the chance that any one worker is getting enough of your content to piece an entire post or article together. Splitting audio files and recombining transcriptions is more work for you, but it is an option.

Now it's time to cover the DIY method for transcribing your work. I won't spend too much time on it, but I do encourage you to give it a shot or 3 to gain some compelling insights.

Transcription DIY Hints

It's time to get funky and listen to you talking to yourself. This can be a little weird at first, but I do have to admit a little secret. When I first transcribed my own work, I was constantly cracking myself up with my little gaffs and mistakes. It was kind of therapeutic to be able to laugh at my own little mistakes and figure out how to fix them next time.

First, you'll need a few tools to help you along the process. A good transcription-geared MP3 playback tool is highly recommended.

VLC Media Player is a nice program that allows a decent level of control over playback speed and supports a wide range of file formats. It's free and works on just about any operating system configuration imaginable. It's not the best as it's geared toward playing media as a main goal, but it works well.

http://www.videolan.org/vlc/

Express Scribe is specifically tuned around transcription and fine playback controls. This might just be the program you need as you'll need to adjust speed on the fly, while scrubbing around the audio file, in order to increase your transcription accuracy.

This program is also free and available for most operating systems. When you visit the website, know that you don't need the foot pedal and there is a 'Free' and 'Free Trial' version available. Get the 'Free' one.

http://www.nch.com.au/scribe/

I recommend these tools because you'll be able to slow down the audio playback. This allows you more time to keep up. Regardless of how fast you type, it can help to have better control over how fast the audio is flying by your ears, especially if the content is confusing or difficult in nature.

As a side note, if you end up enjoying transcription a lot, then you'll be able to save some money over the process and even make some money by doing freelance transcription work. Look to the "sources of outsourcing" section ahead for sites to seek this type of work.

Prepare Your Files and Host Them

If you're doing your own transcriptions, this section (and the next couple of sections) probably won't be too valuable to you at first. I suggest going through them just to be familiar with the process though. You might just be back in time. Let's see what it takes to get some help in the transcription phase now.

You'll need to tackle two main parts here: getting your files edited to an acceptable level and hosting the files for others to access. There are way too many ways to accomplish these tasks to cover in this book, so I will tell you what I use and do along with an alternate suggestion or two.

It's time to clean up your audio files a bit. Hopefully, you won't have to edit them too much as that can eat up a lot of time. There are a few things you need to check and take care of before you make the files live for transcription:

Audio File Cleaning Steps:

1) Chop the dead-air or noisy-air off the beginning ('top it')

2) Chop the dead-air or noisy-air off the end ('tail it')

3) Look for and remove any mistakes or BEEP sections

4) Adjust volume levels, if needed

5) Remove large chunks of dead-air or silence (delete silences >3 seconds)

~~~

This is a good bit of work when you're first starting out, but the editing gets much easier the better you get at dictation. You'll catch on and have a lot less to clean up. Also, really do try to keep your total recording time to 5 minutes as I've only seen much *hate* for longer files. It just seems to be something about 5 minutes as a breaking point or psychological barrier.

If you are a little over 5 minutes, then see if you can scrub through the audio file and remove some more dead-air to get down to the right time. Whatever you do, do *not* try to speed up your audio in order to get it to fit. That only makes things more difficult for the transcriber.

You can also just split the longer recordings into smaller chunks, naming the files in such a way that you'll know they go together later. The transcriber or transcription service will include a filename in the results.

Just find a silent spot half-way through the file, cut and past the last half into a new audio file, and save both with your favorite naming convention. I recommend 'maintopic-xxx**a**.mp3' and 'maintopic-xxx**b**.mp3' as a useful file-naming practice.

As far as programs you can use to do this editing, there is the free Audacity and paid SoundForge. Both work quite well and will do everything you need to get the job done. Here are the links:

http://audacity.sourceforge.net/

http://www.sonycreativesoftware.com/soundforg esoftware

After you've made your edits, it's time to get the files up and on the internet. Depending on the transcription service you end up going with, you may have to upload files to your own preferred destination. However, a lot of the "done for you" transcription companies will have a direct upload feature on their website.

If you end up choosing a service that requires you to host your own files, then the next couple of steps will be useful for you. If you have your own website, then you're good to go already. Just create a new folder on your server, upload the files, and keep note of the URL to get to the transcribers. I highly recommend the free FTP client called FileZilla for doing this.

http://filezilla-project.org/

Ninja Tip: After you upload your files to your server in FileZilla, select them all, left click the highlighted area, and choose "Copy URLs to Clipboard." Ba-da-bing you just saved yourself some time typing all of that out. Yes, you'll need to change the 'ftp://' portion to 'http://' (and maybe pull out a 'www' or so) after you paste it, but this is a nice little shortcut, especially for working in batches. More about batching later.

If you don't have your own server, then you can do just as well with a shared DropBox folder, Google Drive setup, or any number of the many file-sharing services out there. Whatever you do, make sure it's reliable, fast, and easy to access. Now, let's head on over to the sources for this great work.

Sources of Outsourcing

The number of transcription sites popping up on a daily basis is staggering. It's good that more people are catching on to just how useful this type of service is, but how the hee-haw are you to know which one to go with? There are 3 main types of services and I'll cover 3 sites that represent these service types.

To help guide your train of thought over these 3 service types, here are the price ranges you can expect per audio minute:

Outsourcing Sites: $0.25 to $1 per minute
Dedicated Service: $1 per minute
Microtask Sites: $0.15 and up (you set the price)

Fiverr - An Outsourcing Site

The land of getting whatever you want for a mere $5. Sounds too good to be true, right? Sometimes it is and sometimes it isn't. This is the wild-west of the "pay for services" arena and you can get a whole heck of a lot more done here than just transcriptions. Of course, we're focusing on transcription work for now.

This service can be good if you screen out the workers properly. If you just jump in nilly-willy and select a random transcriber, you are most likely going to be disappointed. Here's how I go about finding the best transcribers in this maze of service providers.

Head on over to www.fiverr.com and get ready for some hunting. You can either drill down through the categories to get what you want or enter your best search term in the search box up top. If you know what you're looking for, then I recommend the search box. Let's enter "audio transcription."

BAAM! There you go; over 3,500 results. Time to narrow it down a bit. See the "Show" menu items up towards the top? The "Recommended" option is selected by default. Please oh please click the "High Rating" option instead. You now have all of the results sorted by just how awesome the workers are in the eyes of the customers.

There's only one problem. These are usually the busiest people in the bunch. That comes with being a good service. What I normally do for Fiverr hunting it to open the top 5 to 10 offerings (after sorting by rating) and choosing which one stands out best. Look for delivery time, service samples and images, and any extra offerings that seem useful.

Probably one of the more important things to screen for is the cost per transcribed minute. Look at the maximum number of minutes they are offering to transcribe for the $5. Divide the number of minutes by $5 and you have your cost per audio minute. This is an Outsourcing site and the range should be between $0.25 and $1 per minute.

URL: http://www.fiverr.com/
PROS: cost effective, potential for good workers, can be easy to use, good for single file jobs
CONS: must screen users diligently, potentially long wait times

Ninja Tip: Fiverr can be good for a lot of things, but it can also get you into trouble if you're not careful. For instance, if you decide to use it for ebook covers in the future, make sure to run your image through **TinEye** before paying the freelancer. The last thing you want is to be selling a book with a copyright protected image as your cover.

Speechpad - A Dedicated Service

NOTE: I haven't used Speechpad myself, but the Mixergy Podcast does. Mixergy is a powerhouse of awesome interviews, information, and tons of content. The transcriptions come out quite nicely and I am using this as evidence of Speechpad's validity as a transcription service. Highly recommend the podcast, too. Check it out:

http://mixergy.com/

This service is the total hands-off, upload your files and forget it type of transcription service. The other types of services require quite a bit more human interaction and potential negotiation efforts. Not Speechpad. If you're looking for the easy (but relatively expensive) route, then this may be your best bet.

URL: http://www.speechpad.com/
PROS: easy to use, no real knowledge required, reliable and guaranteed, good for single or multiple file jobs
CONS: high costs, potential for longer wait times

Mechanical Turk - A Microtask Site

Let me start off by saying that no matter which route I end up trying, I always come back to Mechanical Turk (MTurk). This is Amazon's brain-child crowd-sourcing platform that delivers exactly what you ask for at exactly the price you want to pay. This is a Godsend for me, but just plain scary for others.

To tell you the truth, I actually had some hesitation using this platform some time ago. The interface is not intuitive, the setup to get jobs out there is cumbersome, and an accidental change of a setting (like workers per task) can end up costing a lot if you don't catch it in time.

Please, don't let that scare you away. Start with some small task first. Practice with a simple survey asking for answers to 3 simple questions related to your target niche. Get some good market-research data as your practice run. This kind of super short survey can be done for ~$0.05 to $0.10 per answer depending on how generous you're feeling.

Once you cut your teeth on these small jobs, consider jumping up into transcription. I don't really recommend MTurk as your go-to for single file transcriptions, but I wouldn't imagine any other source for batches or multiple file transcriptions. I know we haven't touched on batching, yet, so just keep this in mind for a few more sections.

For now, let me just give you an idea of what can be accomplished with MTurk with one of my own personal scenarios. I create a new batch job on MTurk, set the price for $0.30 to $0.40 per audio minute (depending on several factors), wait for about 07:00 AM CST to release the job, and by early afternoon on the same day all 150 minutes of dictated audio are done and waiting for me to review for a bill of about $55 or so.

Sounds like a lot of money when it's all batched together, right? It's highly affordable and I get awesome results from some highly talented people. Just as a guide, some people outsource article writing and pay $10 per 500 word article, costing $300 for 30 articles. Also, transcribing these 30 files would have cost $150 at Speechpad and would have taken a week.

I'll not bore you further with my obvious love for MTurk and its awesome workers. It has a huge learning curve, but it greatly rewards those looking to harness the power of crowd-sourcing small jobs to create big results.

Ninja Tip: If you post your jobs (HITs in MTurk-speak) at around midnight CST, then you will find plenty of workers happy to work for $0.15 to $0.25 per audio minute. The quality is still pretty good but the results are generally created by workers in countries that aren't as familiar with native English speaking and grammar. You make the call.

URL: http://www.mturk.com/
PROS: very cost effective, blazing fast, unlimited resources, good for multiple file jobs
CONS: very detailed instructions are a must, can be trial and error, complex interface (especially for batching)

~~~

Ready to get a taste of how dictating your content can scale like crazy? Good. Here goes...

TO BATCH IS TO SCALE

Imagine with me here for a minute. You spent 10 minutes setting up your audio recording environment, you have a whole hour instead of just 5 minutes to spare, and you're on fire. Do you just record that 5-minute post and move on your way?

I sure hope not, my friend.

It's time to experience the power of scaling up. With some practice, you can achieve roughly 15 dictated articles in a solid one hour block of time. Yes, a full 15 post of approximately 600 words each, depending on how fast you talk.

That's 9,000 words an hour.
That's roughly 36 single-spaced pages in Microsoft Word.
That's about the length of a special report.
That's about half the length of a small book.
That's about a quarter of the length of a standard nonfiction book.

Think about it. You spend 1 hour of your focused time and you have 1 blog post every other day for an entire month. You spend 4 hours of your time and you've finally written that book you've always wanted to get out of you.

I could go on and I probably will in a future book, but for now we're focusing on creating unlimited small-chunk content. Let's briefly dive into batching your dictations so you can scale your efforts to massive proportions.

Immediate Benefits

Besides the hints and goals I gave in the paragraphs above, you will end up saving a ton of time by batching your work. Think about it for a second. Is it easier to spend the chunk of time setting up your cue cards, your recording studio, and your file processing routine for a single file or for a small group of files?

While you're brainstorming topics, go ahead and make another 14 cue cards. This will take a bit more time, but it's time you were going to spend anyway. You might as well do it while you're in the mood and your brain is fired up.

Also, while you've got the equipment out, grab a glass of water (and maybe a cough drop - drop it in the water for a nice refresher - seriously), and speak out the next 14 articles right then and there. Redoing setup and teardown is minimized, you can strike while your "flow iron" is hot, and you keep the repetition of computer tasks to a minimum.

Plus, you can build a bank of topics to work on so you'll always have something to dictate at the drop of a hat. When I feel like it (or my scheduled blog post count is getting low), then I'll dictate 3 or 4 articles while I'm driving around doing other things. It's nice to have some cue cards ready so I can do this a few days in a row and have another month's worth of posts ready.

Extras On The How-To

Pretty simple stuff here, but I thought a few pointers on how to make batching a bit easier would help out. Most efficiency gains here are boosted with software that can do bulk processing though there are a few tips I've come up with along the way. When in doubt, aim for batches of 15 as it's easy to work in 1 hour chunks.

Batching Tips:

1) Cue Cards: keep doing them in PowerPoint. You can export *all* slides to PNG at the same time.

2) Image Manipulations: exported images not to your liking? No problem. Just change them all at the same time. I highly recommend the free program, FastStone Photo Resizer.

http://www.faststone.org/FSResizerDetail.htm

3) File Renaming: it becomes very important to maintain a proper file-naming system when you're working with batch processing. I recommend something along the lines of "maintopic-xxx.mp3" where xxx is the order of the article in your overall plan. Also, a free utility called "Bulk Rename Utility" is a boon.

http://www.bulkrenameutility.co.uk/Download.php

4) File Conversion: recorded everything in high quality WAV files? Good! It'll be good for your other products, but bad for uploading such huge files. Just use Audiograbber (with the LAME encoder) to convert them all to MP3 in bulk.

http://www.audiograbber.org/

5) Recording Consecutively: no desire to press the stop button between recordings? Me either. Simply beep-out a good 3-5 seconds between each separate piece of content and break them apart in post-production.

6) Cleaning Up Transcriptions: no matter how good the transcriber is, there will be some weird symbols, funky formatting, and slang terms you might want to swap out. Time to open them all up in Notepad++ and do a "Replace in All Open Documents" on them. Piece of cake and it's free.

http://notepad-plus-plus.org/

~~~

If I still haven't convinced you of how awesome batching your dictations is, then I understand. For now, I just ask you plant the seed of batching deep inside and look to try it out in the future. Take a moment now to imagine taking a day off from work, dictating for those 8 hours instead, and having 120 blog posts or 72,000 words of content done and done.

Ninja Tip: Doing batches of several hours can be tough on the vocal cords. Be sure to have plenty of water between each take. Also, warm water with a tablespoon of honey and lemon juice is magical. Same thing for popping a cough drop between takes. I recommend dictating for 25 minutes straight, then take a 5-minute break, and then get right back into another 25 minutes to repeat the cycle.

Don't let technology or technique bog you down. You are capable of so much when you focus your mind to do it. We're done with this section now. Let's figure out what to do with all of this fine content you've been creating.

PART 3

RELEASE AND IMPRESS

IMPORTING AND SCHEDULING

Picture it with me here for a second. You've got a hard drive quickly filling up with a ton of audio files, text files full of transcribed awesome-sauce, and a super-itchy trigger finger ready to release it all.

Do you just press 'go' and have at it? Does your audience or do your readers have expectations for your posting schedule? How long do you want to be able to step away from posting to do other things? These are all important things to consider when it comes to posting frequency.

Frequency Counts

Pop on over to any content marketing blog and you'll find their opinion on how much and how often your content should be released. Is it once a week, once a month, three times a week, or what?

The real answer is: whatever you feel like so long as you're keeping your website alive. I recommend once a week at a minimum just because it keeps readers interested and Google's eyes a bit keener to your site.

I got a bit crazy in the second quarter of 2013 and was releasing 4 to 5 posts per day for a few weeks. Did I get any complaints? No. Did I lose any readers, subscribers, or get *less* traffic? No. Did I get a butt-ton of great content out for people and Google to find quickly? Yes.

Of course, that rate of posting is pretty hard to maintain unless you're recording a steady hour or two per week on a continual basis. That might be a good idea for a new blog, but an established site should probably stick to 1 to 3 posts per week at most.

This brings up an interesting point. When do you want to do this again? When do you want to have to sit down and record or batch out another set of posts? I know it's kind of fun, but this is something you need to plan ahead of time.

If you'd rather not want to have to populate your blog with content for another month, then make sure you release the posts at a rate that will last the month. Have 15 posts going out every other day including weekends. Do the simple math and set it up to get your schedule right.

Again, this leads us into another awesome point. What can you do in the meantime while your blog is on autopilot? Have some other projects to work on? Have a new book to write? Have a new app or script to work on?

You'll be amazed at how freeing it can be to have a constantly updating blog while you go off and do other business-growth actions. This is one step removed from outsourcing your content generation all together, but much cheaper!

On Importing Posts to WordPress

Setting up a blog post from scratch is pretty straight forward. You simply click a few times, paste your new content in, copy that snappy headline in, set the category, do some tags, set the date, and then schedule or post it right away.

Have you ever tried to do that with 10, 20, or 30 posts in a row. Mind numbing madness I tell you. Go ahead and give it a shot the first couple of times, but I recommend getting away from hand importing as quickly as possible.

Earlier in 2013 I found a WordPress plugin called "WP Import" that just about saved my fingers and sanity. All I have to do now is zip my post text files up, upload through the plugin, set the posting frequency, and hit the import button.

10, 20, 30, 100, 500 posts, it doesn't matter. They all get imported in a flash. Also, being able to set the posting frequency by weeks, days, hours, and even seconds is a boon. No need to manually change every single post on a one-by-one basis.

Enough of my gushing on this plugin. But let me tell you, this thing is under $10 and has saved me literally days' worth of time. Check it out on the **book resources page**.

Now that you've got all this great content scheduled up and ready to rock and roll, it's time to make it stand above the rest. Sometimes I wish an "all text" offering is all it took, but going that extra yard can make all the difference in readership loyalty and appreciation.

LOOK AND FEEL

You can be the nicest person in the world, know every cancer-killing cure, and be the best chef known to mankind, but if you look like a mess, then no one will listen. Presentation is an important factor in this new world of short attention spans and tons of options.

Most folks put out decent content and then WordPress takes care of the rest. Sometimes I think we can rely a bit too heavily on automation and it can cause our readership to suffer. While I don't believe you should sink tons of time into perfectionism, you should spend at least a few minutes sprucing up each post or content piece you release.

A couple of tweaks and tips for formatting, added visual appeal, and immersive layers can make a real difference. It's a noisy world out there and you need to turn your hard work into something that'll grab their attention.

A few warnings: this is my personal style of adding flare and visual interest to my posts, handouts, and special reports. Feel free to tweak these tips as you see fit, but they're a good start to set you off in the right direction.

My main goal here is to help you help your readers scan, dive deeper, and stay interested all along the way. Not everyone reads from top to bottom, *or at all*. Work in small chunks, live in small trains-of-thought, and use reading cues to help move the reader along. Here goes.

1) Passing Paragraphs

Keep it to an inch! Yeah, I know that old printed letter rule doesn't work the same way on the monitor as it does on a sheet of paper, but it's a good reminder. Aim for keeping your paragraphs in 3 to 5 sentences groups. From the WordPress post editor, each paragraph should look to be about 4 to 6 lines deep and no longer, depending on how wide you have your browser.

2) Super Sentences

Keep it short and simple. If you're going over the 20 to 30 word mark per sentence, then you probably need to split your sentence up. If you find yourself using a ton of 'ands' or large combinations of commas, then you need to split it up. Aim for short, aim for clarity, aim for readability. This isn't a formal paper. Forget most of what you learned in high school English.

3) Punchy Headings

Always remember that some people will only ever scan or skim your work. It's been said that 80% of people don't continue to read after a shoddy headline. Scary huh? Make every headline, sub-headline, and list heading be punchy, catchy, and to the point. Let the reader get a picture of your content's meaning by just reading the headlines from top to bottom. Have a story in the headlines.

4) Loving Lists

Remember how your posts are broken down into 3 to 7 points? Consider either starting off with or ending up with those 3 to 7 points in a summary list of points. Have any other "bullet-worthy" information in the post? Break it out and make it a list. People love lists more than boring sentences.

5) Pictures, Graphics, & ClipArt, Oh My

Sure, stock photography and clipart screams "I got this at the Microsoft Office ClipArt gallery," but it sure as heck is better than nothing! People want to see visual representations of the ideas you are presenting. I recommend *at least* one interesting (and Pinterest-able) image per post. Oh yeah, make sure it has a meaningful and fun caption. People love captions.

Here are some of the royalty free or creative commons sites that I use when I'm *not* looking for paid-level art:

http://office.microsoft.com/en-us/images/

http://morguefile.com/archive

http://www.flickr.com/creativecommons/by-2.0/

Be sure to check usage rights, though all of the above sites are primarily royalty free resources.

6) Quotes to Live By

What better way to gain some trust and drive your point home than to attach a famous person's awesome quote to your work? Including a punchy and relevant quote or two, set in a fancy "blockquote" via WordPress, can really make the difference between a boring post and a fun one. Please attribute the author.

Just do a trusty Google search and pick one:

+"YOUR NICHE OR TOPIC" +quotes

7) Luscious Links

I know what you're going to say here, but you've got to link up your post. Yes, this even means linking out to a few trusted sources per post. Don't do it just to make me happy, do it because you think it will *help your reader* understand the topic better.

Besides, when is the last time you didn't open an external link in a new window or new tab? Don't worry; your readers aren't going to leave your site. They are going to click over, realize you've helped them out, and come back to you as an even more knowledgeable leader in this niche.

I recommend linking to your own posts or resources at least once as well and at least one external resource, too. Do this for each post. Oh and because you never know what Google will penalize next, please make your external links 'nofollow.' Here's how to add this info in your post's HTML code:

Change: < a href="http://fancyproduct.com">Sponsored Product</a>

To: < a href="http://fancyproduct.com" **rel="nofollow"**>Sponsored Product</a>

Yes, people will be riled up I am recommending this, but it's the safest way to include a link without potentially causing issues to your site later. I've had a useful linked site completely change the page I linked to into a sales page for one of their products. Not cool.

Why make the links 'nofollow'? Well, here's just one example. Google now penalizes sponsored product links that aren't dubbed 'nofollow.' Whether or not you knew this is irrelevant in the eyes of Google. The hammer still swings. Just something to think about.

Okay, okay. Just one more little section to whet your whistle and help you provide an extra level of awesome for your readers, clients, and subscribers. If you thought the above ideas would help you stand out, wait for the next few sections.

Knock 'Em Dead Extras

What if you could provide a whole new way to deliver your content without doing all that much more work? What if you could increase your exposure levels many times over with only a few extra clicks?

Brain researcher Eric Jensen, and every proponent of Neuro-Linguistic-Programming (NLP), is kind enough to point out that there are 3 main ways people like to consume their information:

1) Visual: examples are reading, testing, writing

2) Auditory: examples are lectures, peer review, audiobooks

3) Kinesthetic: examples are adventure learning, physical games, group activities

But often times, we tend to only 'speak' to one of these preferences with our posts, articles, or reports and for good reason, too. It's a lot of work to speak to them all! How often do you want to write a post and then turn around and record yourself reading it just to have an audio version of it available?

But wait... what if you already had an audio version of it available and a cleaned up one at that? Sounds like you'd be ready to make an audio version of your post available. Better yet, you could click just one more button and turn that audio file into a podcast.

Hey, you might as well save that transcription file as a PDF and make it available for download, too, so people can take it on the run. There are a few WordPress "post to PDF" plugins available, too, but I never had any luck with them.

What's that? Amazed that you can record a single 5 minute dictated post and get the following out of it:

1) Blog article
2) PDF download or a bonus for products & subscribers
3) An audio version of the post to supplement your post or include as a separate product bonus
4) A podcast update
5) An audio track for a slideshow YouTube video

~~~

...and many more. Your creativity is really the only thing stopping you from leveraging every second of your life into an infinite number of awesome things to offer your audience. Keep this in mind when you get started. Every bit of awesome content you put out front equals that much more awesome reciprocation and appreciation on the backend.

As long as you keep your mind on providing awesome value to the lives of your readers, clients, and target market, you can bet they will keep coming back for more. There's no shame in optimizing your life to make it easier to help people out. Own it and optimize up, folks.

CONCLUSION

Here's to you never having another "blinky cursor, blank page" Sunday evening ever again. You're now up to speed on the absolute number one fastest (and most effective!) way to create content you know your audience will love.

Bringing in your new ability to find ideas in the most obscure places opens the door for you to create as much content as your vocal cords can handle. Sometimes, the biggest problem can be figuring out how much you want to bug your readers!

You'll achieve long-sought after goals soon with the right frame of mind, the desire to create continual value for the world, and the motivation to know you're only 5 minutes away from a new thought made real. This is a powerful new system.

Commit now to making the Quick Content Formula a go-to tool in your content creation toolbox. The only thing stopping you from being exactly where you're at now and where you want to be is a few blocks of time here and there. Get to recording, get to doing, and get to getting on.

Turn your ideas into thoughts, your thoughts into words, your words into text, and deliver the hee-haw out of your ideas. Here's to your future, my friend.

PS) If anything in this book series is unclear or you want more information, then please email me (or write a letter!) right away. My contact information is a few clicks forward.

About Richard N. Stephenson

I'm the elbow-grease behind richardstep.com, helping thousands discover more about themselves and their career paths daily. I've published several books on career development, personality testing, optimizing learning, and building strengths. I've also designed online self-discovery and career aptitude tests available at richardstep.com.

Cancer once knocked me down, the good Lord gave me a second chance, and now I want to help you use yours. I take the old career development fluff and turn it into tools you can use. I live to make resources that are guaranteed to help you in your career-boosting journey.

I live near Houston, TX, with my extraordinary wife, adorable kids, and overgrown backyard.

Please feel free to contact me. I'm always looking for more career and life enhancing tips.

EMAIL: **mailto:richard@richardstep.com**
TWITTER: **http://twitter.com/rstephenson_**
VIDEOS: **http://youtube.com/rstephensonable**
ADDRESS:
PO Box 3395
League City, TX, 77574-3395

Books by Richard N. Stephenson

See my **Amazon Author page** for my latest books on Amazon: http://bit.ly/rnsamazon

See my **blog author page** for my latest books overall: http://richardstep.com/products/

Your Review Counts!

If you enjoyed this book, or got at least one golden nugget of usefulness out of it, would you mind sharing your experience with the rest of the world, please? A 2 to 3 sentence summary of your thoughts is an awesome gift to others who see it. (I LOVE reading them, too!)

Please leave a review on this book's page at the store you bought it at. Sharing the book link with your friends that could use this information is even better!

It really does help when you share your thoughts and feelings. Plus, I like the idea of my kids coming by my author pages in 20 years and seeing what the world had to say. I am forever grateful!

Thank you,
Richard N. Stephenson

www.ingramcontent.com/pod-product-compliance
Lightning Source LLC
Chambersburg PA
CBHW051812170526
45167CB00005B/1982